FREEDOM
OF THE
SPIRIT

Christopher Titmuss, 45, was an international news reporter working in London, Istanbul, Laos and Australia. In 1970 he was ordained a Buddhist monk for six years in Thailand and India. He now teaches engaged spirituality and insight meditation around the world.

He is the co-founder of various spiritual communities and centres, including Gaia House, an intensive meditation centre in Denbury, Devon, England and the Sharpham North Community, Ashprington, Totnes, Devon.

Christopher is a member and supporter of a number of organizations working for people and planet. He is on the international board of the Buddhist Peace Fellowship. In the June 1987 general election in Britain, he stood for parliament as the Green Party candidate for the constituency where he lives.

This is his second volume of interviews to be published by Green Print. The first volume, *Spirit for Change* was published in 1989.

Christopher Titmuss lives in Totnes with his young daughter, Nshorna.

FREEDOM
OF THE
SPIRIT

MORE VOICES OF HOPE
FOR A WORLD IN CRISIS

Christopher Titmuss

GREEN
PRINT

First published in 1991 by
Green Print
an imprint of the Merlin Press Ltd
10 Malden Road, London NW 5 3HR

ISBN 1 85425 056 6

1 2 3 4 5 6 7 8 9 10: 99 98 97 96 95 94 93 92 91

Typeset by Computerset Ltd., Harmondsworth, Middlesex

Printed by Norhaven Rotation, Viborg, Denmark on environment-friendly paper

Contents

SOCIAL AWARENESS

GLOBAL CONCERNS

Acknowledgements

In 1989 Green Print published *Spirit for Change,* a collection of fourteen interviews with people concerned with engaged spirituality. This second collection of interviews focuses primarily on the inner life, the psychological and spiritual climate, and our relationship to the world.

Between 1985 and 1990 I travelled in France, England, India, Italy, Switzerland, Thailand, the U.S.A. and West Germany to tape these interviews and collect material for this book.

I would like to express my appreciation to all the people I interviewed, who kindly found time in their full schedules. Each person communicated a spiritual awareness and understanding with regard to the issues directly affecting all our lives.

Heartfelt thanks also go to Gwanwyn Williams, who kindly gave much assistance in transcribing many of the tapes, as well as to Evelyn Sweeney and Rose Deiss. Also special thanks to Gill Farrer-Halls for her editing skills.

I also wish to thank various friends who set up several of the interviews for me, including Phra Achaan Dhammadaro, Stephen and Martine Batchelor, Christine Engels, Jim Fowler, Corrado Pensa, James Baraz, Francesca Rusciani and Bhikkhu Pannavudho.

I wish to express appreciation to Jon Carpenter of Green Print who has given continuous support to the publication of both volumes.

To all these people and many more, I am grateful for the opportunity to record and publish these interviews.

May all people, creatures and environment
live in peace and harmony

I wish to express my appreciation to Henrietta Rogell who has worked continuously with me on the typescript. Her help with the editing and with the many details in the preparation of the typescript have been invaluable.

Introduction

Several years ago after giving a public talk on engaged spirituality in Madrid, Spain, I spoke with a very successful and unhappy businessman resident in that city. He had a yacht, a holiday villa on a Mediterranean island and was the owner of several factories and perhaps the largest car in the capital. He told me: 'The purpose of society is to produce and consume. All human activities are subservient to this core idea. There is money to be made in every human activity. Fashion, the latest gadgets, the newest style and subtle refinements of technology ensure the continuity of this momentum. Anybody who protests about these basic values is a threat.'

He went on: 'We live in a society which loves buying and selling, producing and consuming, alcohol, drugs and entertainment. You and your kind will always be regarded as peripheral to the real world. You threaten people's values, jobs, possessions, future, their very reason for existence. You may be tolerated in a democracy but society will take no notice of your spiritual values and your call for a change in priorities.'

Our society has fashioned itself around this 'core idea' that the purpose of life is to produce, consume and acquire. Religion, meanwhile, serves as a peripheral outlet for that spiritual impulse that some claim lies dormant in all human beings. Although certain pleasures are derived from this attitude, it also produces deep unhappiness, confusion and alienation. The spiritual, emotional, psychological and environmental cost of our obsession with getting our own way has to be addressed.

This sobering assessment puts into perspective the immense undertaking involved in the transformation of consciousness. The power of that 'core idea' has contributed to the dissolution of confidence of other societies in themselves. Governments throughout the world have adopted the Western model of economic growth. Societies which were self-supporting and self-sustaining are in widespread decline. The supreme goal of numerous governments is to generate the fastest possible rise in production, distribution, marketing and consumption of goods. Translated into personal terms, this means that the individual works to get what he or she selfishly wants for themselves within the framework of the law.

This philosophy of individualism seems to be triumphing at present. The core idea, centred around producing and consuming for profit, is inseparable from the view that the individual comes first with the mind and body separate from the environment. One French social philosopher recently summed up the situation by saying: 'God is dead. Communism is dying. And I'm not feeling very well myself.' Winner and losers worldwide abound in the competitive forces of the market place.

What is the relationship of any political economic analysis to the spiritual life? The relationship is simply that the core idea is only an idea – admittedly one which has taken root in the hearts and minds of our society. But this idea is not so deep that it cannot be uprooted. Enmeshed around this idea is a whole morass of other views and options. These emphasize a wealth-creating society, competition, the satisfaction of ownership, the striving for success and self-interest for oneself and one's immediate family. This is all that matters. Religious beliefs are just an appendix, providing the consolation of eternal life rather than extinction.

Accompanying this core idea are the emotions of fear and anger. We imagine we own our possessions whereas in fact we are owned by them. The more we have the more we are afraid to lose. We form industries to protect our property. We are constantly strengthening the police force, building more prisons and taking every precaution to protect ourselves and our children.

Nor is there safety and security in our relationships. Relationships break down, families go in different directions and children run away from home. We cannot understand why our loved ones leave us. We feel angry and bitter when things to wrong, when we get into debt or when we are rejected by others. We experience anxiety, boredom, insomnia and insecurity. Owing to a general spiritual and emotional malaise we establish clinics, mental hospitals, gurus, therapists and priests to help alleviate our problems. We then commit the cardinal sin of sending people back to face the core idea still being propagated by society, or we encourage them to withdraw into the comforting arms of an alienated sect.

Social forces and psychological forces cannot be separated from each other. There are those who claim that social forces condition the mind into forms of behaviour. This view suggests that we have to change society, we have to campaign against the dictatorship of the market place and state control. In this view society's obsession with producing and consuming sweeps all along in its wake – like the creatures in the biblical story who blindly rush headlong over the edge of the clifftops.

Others uphold the view that people have to change themselves first. This is but a continuation of the philosophy of individualism. Since the core idea lies within each individual, then each person has to work on themselves, they claim. Each person has to work out their own salvation in order to be free from selfish desire, aggression and fear. Only when people are willing to look into their own lives and see into their conditioned mind can there be real hope of stopping humanity from rushing over the edge.

Perhaps both views – of individualism and of society as a collective – are extremes. The concentration on either extreme hinders us from an understanding that psychological and social forces are not separate from each other. If we work to change society but neglect our own way of living then we are hypocrites. If we are merely engaged in various forms of navel gazing – cherishing of religious beliefs, body work, meditation, psychotherapy, guru devotion – we subscribe to a personal salvation alienated from the totality of life. Both extremes fail to take into account the nature of interdependence of social and psychological factors.

In the spiritual traditions of the East *avidya* (Sanskrit for ignorance, ignoring, blindness, not knowing, not realising) establishes suffering. The solution to *avidya* is *vidya* (knowing, seeing, realizing). *Avidya* and *vidya* are neither bound to the individual nor the collective. Transformation of consciousness occurs in the capacity to say 'no'. That 'no', a potent statement in the language, is directed to whatever is recognized as selfish, violent and unjust. It emerges out of the realization of the harmful if not destructive outcome of unexamined causes and circumstances.

Realization and saying 'no' is a significant step. This ultimate 'no' can touch us so deeply as to become a final statement to the whole package of what is deemed good, whether in the form of the dictatorship of social, inner, political or religious forces. This 'no' empties the heart and mind of taking up both the tyrannies of having or not having a position. It is the dissolution of the entire construction of what is deemed secular or religious. This is not to be interpreted as a nihilistic viewpoint. For the deepest recesses of our being are then awakened to life. There is a profound sense of mystery with an *active* reverence towards expressions of life free from clinging to an ideology. The tyranny of core ideas, whether political, economic or religious, are negated.

It may be that historians will regard the 1980s as a decade that gave greater licence to selfishness. It may be that the 1990s will bring about a call for the values of honesty, integrity, generosity and compassion. We have the reponsibility to examine the quality of our inner and personal lives. We also need to be aware of the way social, economic and political forces impact on our consciousness. I believe we shall need to explore the wide variety of resources available for both inner and outer change. Surely only the naive and the dogmatic will claim that the solution to personal and global issues resides exclusively with a particular person or book or religious, scientific or political standpoint.

To explore actively the relationship between our states of consciousness and the world requires immense dedication. Instead of exploiting the resources of the Earth, its animals and people, we need to make a significant shift in our values. The fields of spirituality, meditation, healing, education, psychotherapy, the arts and nature provide a variety of resources to make insightful changes to our lives. The transformation of consciousness can liberate us from the forces of selfishness. We are becoming too clever for our own good and the good of others. When we are humble enough to acknowledge that we and our leaders do not have all the answers we can explore in a sensitive and respectful way the issues of being alive and active on Earth in these times.

This book is a series of interviews with five women and ten men on themes of engaged spirituality. Each interview consists of an inquiry into psychological or social forces and ways we may explore our perceptions and experiences of circumstances that affect us. Each of the interviewees questions the harmful forces that bring suffering to people's lives.

What is communicated by each is the willingness to take risks, to raise difficult questions on the accepted way of things and to explore the potential for change through words and actions. As with my first volume of interviews, it is unlikely that all those interviewed in this volume would agree with each other in all perceptions of what matters. What is apparent is their capacity to communicate their concerns and insights through a variety of ways. I have benefited considerably from my contact with such people, several of whom are friends.

There is a two-fold intention behind this book. Firstly, it provides us with some direct insights into ourselves and the world we live in. Secondly, it may serve as an inspiration to engage in that noble human activity of exploration into the nature of things and service to others.

This collection of interviews is primarily an examination of the significance of our inner life in relationship to social and global realities. In the application of such concerns we express that spiritual impulse that simultaneously reveals a reverence for life and that remarkable freedom of a human being to transcend conditioning.

We dwell in this period of history when for the first time the fragility of the ecosystem is being revealed to us day in and day out. May this book and other such communications contribute to our awareness and realization of this inexplicable presence we participate in that is full of wonder.

Christopher Titmuss
Totnes, Devon, England
In the time of fallen leaves, 1990

INNER AWARENESS

Human beings are conditioned

An interview with J. Krishnamurti
Brockwood Park School, Hampshire, England

Jiddu Krishnamurti was born on 11 May 1895 at Madanapalle, 150 miles north of Madras, India. He was the eighth child in the family. His father, also named Jiddu, was employed by the British as a rent collector. One evening the boy was sitting on the beach with some other children when a theosophist named Charles Leadbeater picked him out to be the World Teacher.

In January 1911 an order called the Order of the Star was formed by leading theosophists, with Krishnamurti put at its head. He was 16 years old. He stayed in England from 1912 to 1920, living with privileged families, learning and being exposed to Western culture. His brother Nitya accompanied him everywhere. In 1925 Nitya died, leaving Krishnamurti heartbroken and disillusioned.

In time, Krishnamurti recovered. Sobered and strengthened by the experience, in July 1926 he began leading small camps. Three years later at the Star camp, in the presence of 3,000 Star members, Krishnamurti dissolved the order.

He began his talk that day with words that are familiar to those who have ever listened to him or read his books: 'I maintain that Truth is a pathless land.'

He went on to say, 'I do not want to belong to any organization of a spiritual kind . . . You have been accustomed to being told how far you have advanced. How childish! Who but yourself can tell if you are incorruptible?'

The theme of that talk ran through every talk that Krishnamurti gave from the time he dissolved the order and resigned from the theosophists until the day he died. Throughout his life he continued to give public talks around the world, hold camps, initiate a number of small, progressively-minded schools, have a wide range of his talks and dialogues published and videos made available.

I first began listening to Krishnamurti in 1968 when a friend in Sydney, Australia gained access to a number of his taped talks. I attended his talks several times in India and I remember how much the people in his audience were coughing and spluttering due to colds and chills, if not from tuberculosis.

In 1982 and 1983, I had lunch with him a couple of times at Brockwood Park School in Hampshire. I sat opposite him. He began his meal by eating a single red apple which he placed in the centre of his plate and afterwards a little vegetable and salad. He asked me what I thought of India. 'You can say anything you like. I'm not Indian, you know.' I told him of the poverty, violence and corruption I saw; I mentioned the beauty, the religious life and the capacity of India to touch one deeply. He agreed. He told me that when he was a young man he had spent many years out of India. Upon his return he was so saddened by what he saw that he spent his first week back in India in bed.

In October 1984 friends teaching at the school arranged for me to have an hour-long meeting with Krishnamurti who was now in his 89th year. To say that this was a difficult interview would be to put it mildly. It seemed ironic that part way through the meeting the tape recorder broke down and so the conversation was interrupted for a few minutes while the machine was fixed.

I decided to explore the field of meditation with him. Frequently, he cut me off as I was talking. He was impatient in his tone and continued to put forward views. It was not that I disagreed with what he said but the difficulty was more in his tone of speaking.

I'm sure he didn't want to speak as the final authority but that, unfortunately, was the impression left. In a rather fatherly way, he would place his hand on top of mine from time to time – which admittedly softened the impact of being cut off in mid-sentence. With the end of his life approaching I suspect that Krishnamurti was experiencing some frustration and disappointment about whether he had ever been understood in his terms. I know a number of us who met with him over the years or listened to him speak were profoundly influenced by him. I wonder how much he realized this.

After the meeting, he got up, we shook hands and he walked briskly to the door. Then, almost as an afterthought, he turned to me, smiled and said, 'I hope we shall meet again.' It was one of his last private interviews.

He continued to give public talks until his final talk in Madras, India in January 1986, the area where he was discovered 75 years earlier. Krishnamurti told his audience that this might be his last talk, although hardly anybody realised what he was saying. He flew back to Ojai, California. He was dying. Two weeks later, just two days before his death, he asked to be taken outside in a chair. Once outside, he placed both hands together and bowed in all the directions to the beautiful nature surrounding him. He was 90 years old. After he died, his ashes were scattered in different parts of the world.

I'm grateful that the interview took place. He was human, after all.

CT: I want to express my appreciation for the opportunity to meet with you today. I have looked forward to this for a long time. I would like to discuss and explore with you the field of meditation. It is an area of life in which I am involved.

K: You are only concerned with meditation?

CT: I'm concerned with other areas. One of the questions which arises with frequency is the question of meditation with form, structure, method and technique as emphasised in many Eastern traditions. Your emphasis is that meditation must be free . . .

K: Right from the beginning, what do you mean by the word 'meditation?'

CT: I make this concept interchangeable with such concepts as 'observation', 'mindfulness', 'total attention'. I use the word 'meditation' in a broad way.

K: I'm asking what the word conveys, not the structure of meditation.

CT: What the actual word conveys?

K: The etymological meaning of the word.

CT: It means to give care and attention to the here and now.

K: We are not meeting each other. As I understand looking into the various dictionaries, it means 'to ponder over', 'to think over'. The word in Sanskrit, I believe, means 'to measure'. It is merely a process of measurement.

CT: A measure of what?

K: What is, what should be, what one might achieve, what has been.

CT: And this comes within meditation itself?

K: We'll pry into the question 'what is meditation?' not 'how to meditate'. We will not go into the various systems whether they be Buddhist, Hindu, Tibetan or of any other guru who has a particular system of meditation. We are not discussing for the moment which is correct but what meditation itself is.

The meaning of the world implies constant endeavour, constant self-recollectedness, constant observation of what one is doing, what one is not doing, attention to one's body, the movement of the body, the controlling of thought and forcing thought to hold itself. All of this is implied in all of the systems, whether it is Zen Buddhism, or Tibetan, or even Christian contemplation. There is a sense of effort that is involved.

CT: The application of attention using effort is to give care and attention to thought.

K: All of that is implied. That is generally understood as meditation. I can include what you do in all of this. There is the whole Zen system, awareness, sitting up very still and having quieted the mind, controlling every reaction.

CT: I would say that the element of control certainly comes in because . . .

K: Of course, of course.

CT: But that is the *initial* expression due to the unfamiliarity of sitting still for varying periods of time.

K: So the central factor of meditation, yours or others, is to control, in the sense of to hold.

CT: Yes, but that is a certain stage within the scope of . . .

K: That is measurement. That is why the word 'meditation' implies 'measurement', the beginning and the end.

CT: Isn't it quite often that the individual enters into a new area such as meditation and, given his or her conditioning, says, 'I am going to meditate in order to come to somewhere else'?

K: Yes, generally, that is what is understood.

CT: That initial understanding of meditation may change as a person's understanding of meditation changes.

K: Yes, that is all measurement. 'I do not understand but I will understand. I am "this", whatever "this" is and I will come to "that" which is a time interval.' All that is an effort.

CT: Are you implying here that by establishing a measurement it in some way . . .

K: I'm observing, not condemning, agreeing or changing. I'm clearly seeing that in meditation, those practising meditation, taking various postures cross-legged or whatever, there is the element of time, measurement, control and something to be achieved. These are the central factors in all meditation.

CT: I get an underlying feeling that it is inappropriate . . .

K: I will tell you exactly that there is no underlying hidden something. There are the various factors of meditation which you and the others pursue. We never ask, 'Why should I do all of this? Why should I meditate?' We do exactly the same thing in other directions. 'I am a poor man and I want to become a rich man.' 'I don't know but I will know.' 'I am a clerk and I want to become an executive.' 'I don't know how to drive a car but give me three weeks' time and I will learn it.' It is the same movement.

CT: Yes, but there is a qualitative difference.

K: It is the same movement. You are trying to call something 'spiritual', right?

CT: Yes . . .

K: There, it is mundane. It is worldly. It is necessary. One asks for money, for shelter, therefore it is necessary. There is also a certain discipline there. Here too I must have discipline.

CT: But within . . .

K: I'm not condemning anything. I'm just watching.

CT: So you are pointing out that there are two major parallels between one movement of mind which is . . .

K: No parallel. They are exactly the same.

CT: They are exactly the same in terms of the movement of the mind.

K: The clerk says, 'Give me another ten years and I'll be manager.' Here, too, 'I'm the beginner and I'll come to the top,' which is illumination. What is the difference between these two?

CT: I feel there is a certain difference. I don't wish to exaggerate the importance of the relativity of inner development.

K: It is exactly the same thing, only you call that 'spiritual', 'inner'. This is psychological, subjective, under the skin; the other is done in a factory.

CT: I would think that the difference is that in spite of the identical nature of the two, one may contribute towards inner change and the other may deny it.

K: The other doesn't deny it. I've changed. I have a better house, a better garden. We have extended that same ambition to this so-called spiritual world.

CT: There is certainly an enormous danger in this transference from one kind of world into the other.

K: They are both the same. If I come to you and you tell me to meditate I would reply that I don't know what you mean by that. You tell me to investigate, to pay attention to what I am doing. These are all things that you and others say. Right?

CT: Yes. Hopefully one communicates the actual position one is in at the present time.

K: What does that mean?

CT: That may mean that a person is experiencing frustration, confusion or pain. It means that the primary emphasis initially . . .

K: Not primary or secondary. Let's look at what you are saying. I'm not criticising you. I'm just observing what you are saying. Primary, the beginning. And with the beginning there is an end. That's what all of the gurus, all of the Eastern philosophers are saying: 'Begin and you will get it. You will come near it.'

Pursuing this logically, I can find a rationale for all of this. In the same way I have to live in this beastly society so I must have more money otherwise I would be destroyed. And one looks at that . . .

CT: And sees there is a certain emptiness to it.

K: That's it. Empty, right? Here if I do certain things I won't be empty. I'm not criticising anything. I will tell you what I think presently.

CT: As I listen to you what comes to mind is a condition of a number of people who find it extraordinarily difficult to make a leap which leaves behind their relative conditioning. What we have been describing is a material pursuit and a spiritual pursuit which certainly implies a beginning but it may not imply an end.

K: Forgive me, but you are repeating the same thing. That's what they all say, the Tibetan Buddhists, the Hindus, the gurus.

CT: Does the fact that something is repeated undermine it or disqualify it?

K: No, certainly not.

CT: By repeating I am trying to acknowledge the reality of those individuals' conditioning.

K: Human beings all over the world are conditioned as Christians, Buddhists, scientists, doctors, gurus. They are all conditioned by their culture. Those people who meditate and those who don't meditate are all conditioned by their culture.

CT: Is it a total form of conditioning, though?

K: That's the question. Is there within the human condition a part of an inward state where there is no conditioning – a small part? Is that what you are saying?

CT: Is there a small part that isn't conditioned? It does seem that given a certain outlook and attitude on life, we can look at mental processes clearly and directly, inwardly and outwardly. Therefore my question is: Are there beneficial conditions for this kind of receptivity?

K: You'll have to re-word your question, sir. What do you mean by 'condition'?

CT: The bringing together . . .

K: I'm asking what do you mean by the word 'condition'? The meditator is conditioned.

CT: Does the fact that the meditator is conditioned blind the meditator to a consciousness where one *can* see clearly?

K: That means he must be free of conditioning.

CT: At least not overwhelmed by it.

K: No. Isn't your question about the whole brain, which is after all the only instrument we have? The brain is all the reactions, the responses, the neurological patterns, ambitions, greed and envy. You are asking what is the conditioning that will help to free the brain of its conditioning. Are you sure you are asking that question?

CT: I think I'm conceited enough to think I know the answer. My question is: Isn't there an element of mindfulness of observation within our brain which is able to see our mental processes clearly and directly?

K: So then we have to go into the question of observation, of seeing clearly. What do you mean by 'seeing'?

CT: An awareness . . .

K: You see, I am not totally ignorant of your words. Don't put me into 'awareness' and all that. What do you mean by 'seeing', 'observing'? I observe that sofa. The visual observation, the whole window, the colour, what she [my daughter, Nshorna, playing on the floor] is doing. That is observation. The reactions are verbal, 'bright', 'dark', 'black'. So in that observation there is a verbalization of which one can also be aware. This is what is happening. 'That is green.' 'That is a child.' Remembrance and recognition. Then there is organization and representation. So these operate all the time, of course.

CT: Someone has an experience of seeing and they are affected by that experience.

K: Who is it that is being affected?

CT: In my use of language I would say that consciousness is affected by the field of mental experience. Moods, feelings, thoughts affect consciousness. One also identifies, for example, with eye consciousness in its connection with the field of vision. 'I' see.

K: What is 'consciousness?'

CT: The element of being conscious.

K: I am conscious of that chair.

CT: And in that there is a relationship formed between the element of consciousness . . .

K: So you would say that 'consciousness' is its whole content. It is not just some content, including, memories, reactions, fears, pleasure, pain, depression.

CT: But given our moment to moment existence the content . . .

K: . . . changes, varies. But there is still content within this area which we call 'consciousness'. Whether small or big, that is not important. All of the physical, biological, elements, reactions, responses, memories, tendencies, fear, sorrow, pain, depression, aspiration, envy, Britishness, 'I'm British,' 'I'm Indian.' All of that is in my consciousness.

CT: Right. In the form of language that you are using here you are making the consciousness and the content totally identical.

K: The consciousness as we know it is non-existent.

CT: Certainly one cannot have a separate existence from the other.

K: I didn't say the 'other'. You are saying the 'other'. I take an ordinary person; his consciousness is what he is, what he thinks, what he feels, what his aspiration is. He believes in God, he is a Catholic, non-Catholic, Protestant, Hindu, Buddhist. His own tendencies, his longings, his loneliness, his despair – all that is his consciousness.

CT: That is a condition of the consciousness.

K: This is *his* condition.

CT: Within the condition of the consciousness . . .

K: That is *his* consciousness. There is no other consciousness. You can invent another consciousness, superconsciousness, but you are still within consciousness.

CT: It is not a point which is clear to me because in looking, for example, at the chair, it is going too far to say the consciousness is the chair. The chair is an object in consciousness.

K: Of course.

CT: That object in consciousness means that there is a stated relationship which is there. Does that not apply equally to the whole scope of the mind experience?

K: So I'm seeing the whole brain as conditioned.

CT: Yes.

K: This conditioning is its consciousness, right?

CT: Yes.

K: So if one is born in India one's consciousness contains all of the beliefs, superstitions, blah, blah, blah. If I'm born in a Roman Catholic family it contains all the beliefs of Jesus, blah, blah, blah. This is conditioning. It is not one form of conditioning. They are both conditioned.

CT: I agree.

K: Now you come along and say, 'Look, meditation is necessary to uncondition.'

CT: Not necessarily to uncondition but to find clarity with regard to the events that are happening.

K: That's very simple. Clarity of what is happening. In the meeting between political leaders they are playing games. One is playing a political game to get elected and the other is definitely concerned about his opinions. You don't have to hear what they are going to say.

CT: No, it's quite apparent.

K: So we are moving away from the central fact that human beings are conditioned. They are programmed like computers. It is obvious. And human beings have been wanting and searching for something spiritual, what you call 'religion'. There have been people who have been saying, 'Yes, there is something there called spiritual, religious.' It's been going on for a million years. Now you come around and say, 'To find that, meditate,' to put it crudely. I can put it more subtly if you want.

CT: I prefer subtlety.

K: All right. To teach that sublime thing, the brain must be tranquil. They say the same thing, the Buddhists, the Zen, the Hindu. The Christians haven't gone into this very deeply, the others have. Then the problem arises: Who is it that is going to make it silent? Who is the controller that controls thought? We never ask that question. We say that we must control thought.

CT: With inner observation . . .

K: 'Inner observation' – what do you mean by that?

CT: Meaning in this case sitting alone or . . .

K: Why should I do that when I can do it much more simply? In my relationship to my wife or husband I watch my reactions there.

CT: But one doesn't exclude the other.

K: I begin there. I begin to see my relationship – the whole structure of myself. I don't have to ask you to teach me how to meditate.

CT: One certainly doesn't have to go . . .

K: That is what is happening in the world. You have become the guru. I am not being insulting, please.

CT: That is an insult.

K: So I would say, don't go through all this process of meditation and all of that. You have a very good opportunity to learn about yourself, know yourself, which is your relationship with nature, to your wife, to the politician, to your neighbour to whom you are talking. You can be aware of all of your reactions. Then go further. I don't need anybody to tell me how to go. That's my interest. I want to find out.

CT: Certainly that must be the major emphasis.

K: That is the only emphasis, not major.

CT: OK, but given the . . .

K: Not OK. That is the only thing I can begin with because I'm related to everything all my life.

CT: If I may say, people within the pressure of the social reality find it is . . .

K: . . . impossible.

CT: Exactly.

K: That means that you haven't understood society and your relationship to society. You have created this awful corrupt society because you are all like that.

CT: If the person is generally floundering within it then . . .

K: Stop.

CT: Stop what?

K: This floundering. You see it is so simple. Someone sits up and says, 'I'll help you.' This game has been going on for a million years. Somebody, the priest, the psychiatrist are all trying to help. Therefore you are making the listener whom you are helping weak. Everything you find out. Don't depend on anybody.

CT: That is an indispensable emphasis – to encourage . . .

K: I don't want that. You see how you are using these words. I don't want to encourage anybody. I don't want to help anyone. I say, 'Look, it is right in front of your nose, the whole world and yourself in relationship to the world. There is something much greater than that. Go into it.' Why should I be a leader? Historically, how many leaders have we had?

CT: I am completely with you.

K: Sir, you talk about meditation. I say any form of conscious meditation is no meditation.

CT: That is tough language.

K: It is desire that is making me sit. It is desire that says I must achieve.

CT: Can't the desire . . . ?

K: You haven't come to what is desire. What is the nature of desire? Please, meditation is something entirely different, not all of this intellectual or emotional effort. This is something that must be done – not 'must be done'. Something which is consciousness with all of its travail, with all this anxiety, pain, loneliness. All that must be understood first. That's the corruption – not pornographic books and drugs. Corruption is when we are selfish, arrogant, envious. Begin there. Start there.

A life of mindfulness

An interview with Meichee Patomwon Indanno
Supanburi, Thailand

By any measurement, whether religious or secular, Meichee Patomwon has led an unusual life. She was born in a village in the province
of Nakornsridhammaraj in southern Thailand in October 1944. At
the age of twelve she decided to leave her parents, brothers and sisters
and become a Buddhist nun.

She entered a monastery and underwent ordination. Her ordination included the taking of a number of precepts, including the vows
to not kill living beings, not to engage in sexual activity and not to
take any food between the hours of noon and daylight the following
day.

Upon ordination her head and eyebrows were shaved – as they
have been every full moon since then – and she donned the white
robes of the nun of the Theravada tradition. To all intents and
purposes, it was saying good-bye to her past, her parents and her
future in the lay life. She was given the name Meichee which means
ordained spiritual sister.

During her late teens she came to prominence in Thailand through
a specific incident. While meditating one day, she recalled what she
was convinced was her past life. The experience of her death as a child
in her last life was so clear that she knew which village and which
house she died in, although she had never been to the village before.
She decided to visit the village and talk to the people in the house.
When she finished describing what happened to her, to their astonish-
ment, they confirmed all the events that took place the year before
Patomwon's birth. News of this got out to the media and was widely
reported.

In 1963, she became a meditation disciple of the Ven. Achaan
Dhammadaro, probably Thailand's foremost vipassana (insight)
meditation teacher. She practised meditation under his guidance at
Wat Chai Na monastery, outside the main town of the province of
Nakornsridhammaraj, and she has lived there ever since. She is now a
highly respected teacher of vipassana meditation in southern Thailand and a public speaker on spirituality. In 1984, she was appointed
head nun of the province.

Besides the discipline of being a nun, Meichee Patomwon has lived under the rule of having no physical contact whatsoever with a man even in the mildest form, whether shaking hands or when seated on a bus.

From 1970 to 1973 I lived in Wat Thao Kot as a monk. Meichee Patomwon and the other nuns lived on one side of the monastery while the monks lived on the other. I would see her occasionally in the dining hall in the mornings or in the teacher's room for dialogue. Occasionally the teacher, Achaan Dhammadaro, Meichee Patomwon and a handful of other monks and nuns and myself would travel to one part of the province to give teachings. It was a time of much terrorism in this area, some fifteen hours on the train south of Bangkok.

I couldn't help but notice Meichee Patomwon's remarkable spiritual presence. Although she finished her education at the age of eleven and never took up any schooling again, she speaks with an unusual degree of eloquence. Being slim, bright-eyed and beautiful, her life could easily have been dedicated to values utterly different from those of a nun.

In February 1988 I paid my first visit back to Thailand for twelve years. Once again I made the train journey to Nakornsridhammaraj and to the monastery where I had spent time. I did not know whether she was still living there or even whether she was still ordained. I walked into the teacher's room only to see her sitting there with two other nuns. Meichee Patomwon didn't appear to have changed at all since the early seventies.

Through an interpreter I told her that I would like to record an interview with her. The interview was held outside in the shade of a fruit tree. She brought with her another nun, as is customary in Thailand. A monk or nun in this religious discipline never spends time even in a public place alone with a member of the opposite sex.

The interpreter for the interview was Bhikkhu Pannavuddho. He was a novice and monk from the ages of fourteen to twenty-four. He then left the monkhood to marry and had two sons. Two years ago he was re-ordained as a monk; his two sons, now aged ten and thirteen, are ordained as novices and his wife is ordained as a nun. Pannavuddho's elderly parents were also ordained more than ten years ago.

With some people, presence speaks as loud if not louder than words. Meichee Patomwon is such a person.

CT: You have spent many, many years as a nun. What do you

regard as being the most important thing in life?

MP:　The most important thing in life is to practise the Dharma. Dharma means to practise and apply to life the four foundations for mindfulness and awareness in life; that is, to be aware of body, feelings, thoughts and the nature of things. What is necessary for all people is to have mindfulness and clear comprehension of all our activities all of the time throughout our life.

CT:　Why do you consider this so important for human life?

MP:　Unless we live with mindfulness and awareness, we are likely to live in error, to make many mistakes. Anyone who lives with mindfulness of body, feelings, thoughts and the nature of things protects themselves from much unnecessary suffering and pain in life. Without mindfulness we do not live with intelligence, either inwardly or outwardly.

CT:　I can see that mindfulness and awareness are beneficial for oneself and others but what is specifically spiritual about such a way of life? We can be very mindful when dressing, eating, reading, driving and so on.

MP:　A common denominator of people all over the world is being mindful of their activities but this mindfulness is an ordinary kind of mindfulness, a conventional mindfulness. But one must realise the nature of the object of mindfulness. One must penetrate into things through mindfulness and awareness.

CT:　You are saying that there is one kind of mindfulness useful for daily life and another depth of mindfulness that realises the nature of phenomena, that realises the Dharma. Please speak more about this second kind of mindfulness.

MP:　Both expressions of mindfulness are right mindfulness but the second kind is a noble expression of right mindfulness in order to observe deeply the way things are. Everytime we move the body or when it is still, we direct the mindfulness to the body in a sustained way. We experience directly what is occurring on a moment to moment level. When I am established in the body, whether moving or still, there is peace of mind and contentment in that mindfulness. Mindfulness is learning to be in touch with the body and be friends with the body.

CT:　If we observe and stay in touch with the body then suffering will go out of the body?

MP: In this body unsatisfactoriness constantly is arising and passing. When I penetrate into the body, the suffering in the body dissolves and peace pervades. What also occurs is that wisdom or understanding emerges in the mind with regard to suffering. What is necessary here is patience along with awareness so that we continue to look at the body and its suffering. Unless there is patience with the practice of mindfulness the suffering will not stop.

CT: You have practised mindfulness meditation for many years. You are a nun since you were twelve years of age. You have shaved your head every month. As a woman, how do you view your body today?

MP: I have no problem with the body. I see the unsatisfactoriness arising and passing in the body but there is a genuine happiness in the mind when being aware of 'my' body.

CT: This is rather hard to understand. You see the body and its unsatisfactoriness and the mind is happy. Why isn't the mind unhappy?

MP: Before finding this real happiness in relationship to the body, we must meet suffering first. If someone wants to earn money they have the responsibility to work first to earn that money. When we regard the body as an opportunity to practise the Dharma, then the mind and body can work together. But if we are constantly afraid to look directly at the body, just as it is, we can never find wisdom or joy in relationship to it. We must see body as body and not avoid it or deny it.

CT: Do you experience any rejection of the body when you are mindful of it?

MP: When we see suffering with regard to the body we must be able to face it. If we cannot face our experience we will not be motivated to find the end of it and so we reject the body. I have realised the happiness of not grasping onto the body, not adhering to it, not feeling stuck with the body. I know the joy of seeing into the body directly.

CT: So your heart and mind is comfortable with your body?

MP: Yes. The mind is very comfortable with the body.

CT: Let us turn our attention to the mind. After years of observation of the mind, its feelings and thoughts, what changes have you seen in yourself over the years?

MP: Through observing the mind, wisdom arises. The practice has given me insight about myself and I am able to let go of suffering when it arises.

CT: But why does wisdom come from observing the mind?

MP: The insight and understanding that comes reveals that all I call 'myself' consists of body, feelings, perceptions, thoughts and consciousness. The wisdom about 'myself' cures the problems in the mind. When we go along with the defilements and problems in the mind we will experience conflict with them. But once we have decided to really look at these patterns and go through any conflict with them, we can cure the mind of its suffering.

CT: Besides the observation of 'oneself' and the discovery of wisdom and joy in the clear comprehension of mind-body, is there anything else which is significant in life?

MP: Yes. Other things in life are important besides mindfulness. There is the necessity for an ethical foundation for life and a depth of meditation and wisdom. All give support to mindfulness. We then go even more deeply within so whatever is held by the mind in a particular way as being 'me' or 'mine' is given up and is regarded as a false view.

CT: After some thirty years of spiritual practice don't you find it boring to observe mind-body? Is it boring to sit or walk in meditation and be mindful moment to moment?

MP: I don't find it boring at all. In fact, I hope to continue the practice for the rest of my life. All the other things of life are simply to make practice possible.

CT: Has this mindfulness and understanding altered your general perceptions of life and the world? When you open your eyes does the world look different in any way because of all this practice?

MP: I regard the pursuit of things in the world as full of suffering and unsatisfactoriness. There is no real benefit anywhere in this way of living. People must learn to understand life and not be attached to having so many things from the world. This attachment brings suffering to the whole world. I see that my life continues for the purpose of working to bring benefit to other people. All that I can do is to help people come to an understanding of the Dharma of life.

CT: Some people, when they become aware of the suffering in this world, become very unhappy with what they see. I know you are not unhappy, but why doesn't the state of the world make you feel unhappy?

MP: People who do not practise meditation keep thinking of the world as separate from themselves and become unhappy. When we see the true nature of things, we do not feel unhappy.

CT: To be mindful and live with wisdom is the same as living without attachment. Is that right?

MP: The more one grasps onto anything, the more suffering is experienced. The less grasping there is, the more happiness is experienced. My practice is to be free from every trace of impurity of mind and to live with deep friendship and loving kindness for all beings.

CT: Why does loving kindness and friendship come from mindfulness?

MP: I want people to discover this happiness that comes from mindfulness and awareness. I want them to meet this happiness just as I have met it in myself. There is a friendship which comes but also compassion. One's heart does not want to see anyone suffering any more, although one cannot force people to live with mindfulness. At times one has to keep silence. When people reject mindfulness, they continue to experience confusion and pain. One feels compassion for such people.

CT: What do liberation and freedom mean to you?

MP: I regard freedom in terms of the absence of unhealthy or unsatisfactory patterns. Liberation is found from one day to the next. I have no concerns about the future. It is enough to live one day at a time. We can discover freedom immediately and live in freedom in our daily life. The interactivity of body, feelings, perceptions, thoughts and consciousness appears and passes, and nothing else is going on outside of them.

CT: How do you experience being the head nun, a meditation teacher and public speaker on the Dharma? Do you have less time now to observe yourself?

MP: Responsibility for others makes no difference to the opportunity to see into oneself. The mind stays light when we live mindfully.

CT: I notice that the women practise very hard in the monastery — harder than any of the monks, in fact.

MP: Women are very aware of the fact of suffering in life. This motivates women to practise continuously.

CT: Many nuns and monks ordain for a short period of time. They leave the monastery and go back to get married and have children.

You have seen this happen many times over the years. Do you think at times that by being a nun you might be missing something?

MP: Actually [*laughing*] I feel that people who get lost in *things* are missing something. They are missing the realization of completion here and now. To know completion is what matters. Life is complete through realizing ethics, meditation, wisdom and freedom.

CT: How does a nun become a teacher?

MP: The nun must have depth of experience and understanding to be ready to teach.

CT: Do you have the authority to make somebody a teacher or do you have to approach Achaan Dhammadaro for permission?

MP: It is not necessary to approach the Achaan. Some people want to teach but cannot. It is like somebody wanting to teach others how to swim but they cannot swim themselves. We can realize *nirvana* in this practice. *Nirvana* means cessation, not a death but the cessation of grasping and attachment. I want everybody to enter into spiritual practice for the welfare of oneself and the whole world. Then a genuine and abiding happiness will be found in the world.

CT: Listening to you, Patomwon, brings a joy to my heart. Kop Khun mahk [Thank you very much].

Nightmares in New York

An interview with Norman Rosenburg
Totnes, Devon, England

Norman Rosenburg, co-author of the *The Healing Sea*, works as a psychotherapist, Reichian therapist and meditation teacher in the heart of New York. It is a city where tension, anxiety and ambition dominate millions of people's lives. Thousands of psychotherapists are attempting to cope with the daily nightmares of countless numbers of New Yorkers.

He travels regularly to Europe with his wife, Leeny Sack, to co-teach retreats at Gaia House in Devon and in Austria. He told me: 'Living in New York is a constant challenge. On the best day when you fly in you see this brown haze hanging over Manhattan. I get sick for two days after I have been away from the city. My body has literally to switch over from breathing poison.

'We are living in this incredibly compressed space in Manhattan with the noise pollution and people pressure. My wife, a teacher of kinetic awareness, my former wife, Laura Rosenburg and I decided to open a retreat centre in upstate New York on 23 acres of pasture and woodland for people from the City to spend time.'

Norman Rosenburg has adopted unusual methods in his 'interviews' with clients. Firstly, he does not set an hourly fee but relies on clients to give a donation. His sessions are likely to be conducted sitting on the floor or in a restaurant or in the park. He encourages his clients to meet regularly together with his other clients and himself as a group. His unorthodox methods develop a great deal of trust between him and his clients which serves as the raw material for developing insight into each person's situation.

Norman was born in Brighton Beach, Brooklyn, New York in 1941. By the time he was fifteen years of age he had entered New Mexico Military Institute with a view to a career as a soldier. He then went on to study psychology at Ohio State University and at Aberdeen University in Scotland.

He was one of a number of Jews who travelled to Israel at the time of the Israeli-Egyptian war in 1967. He then returned to Scotland and married Laura. They were married for sixteen years. They divorced, re-married and then both agreed that they started to make the same mistakes again. Rather than risk their close friendship, they divorced once more.

Norman later married again. His wife Leeny and his ex-wife Laura are very close friends. Norman said: 'Laura is the closest family member that I have in the world. She is now my sister. The three of us meet together regularly.'

Norman and Laura lived in Israel from 1970 to 1973. Although from a Jewish background and a trained soldier, Norman made many friends who were Arabs or Jordanians. 'Laura and I had friends on both sides. I knew I couldn't fight on either side. I didn't know how to sit in the middle of the conflicts. So at that point we left.'

In New York he began writing poetry and stories about the sea. He then spent several years living alone in the woods in New York State with his cats. It was during this period that he explored the processes of meditation. Upon his return to New York he began to receive clients. During the 1980s he and his wife, Leeny, began to receive invitations from several European countries to teach retreats and workshops.

This interview is an exploration of his methods and of his concerns about the state of mind of people living in a goal-orientated society, where personal achievement is God.

CT: You work as a psychotherapist in New York. New York is intense, aggressive, stressful. What kind of clients to you work with?

NR: The words 'stressful' and 'aggressive' do not really describe New York. New York is desperate. It has a meanness to it that makes the people who come to me desperate for warmth, a place where they can at least be heard and, if a miracle happens, understood.

CT: What makes New York desperate?

NR: People are constantly competing with each other in a hard, cold, cut-throat way and this is accepted as a fact of life here. No matter what profession you are talking about, this is what you find, with rare exceptions. The competition for affordable living space is also fierce. And the number of enormously talented people trying their luck here is very high. No matter how good you are at what you do, here you're just one more blade of grass on the lawn. Despite your talent, you might not get a chance. That's frightening.

CT: So, your clients share the feeling of 'not getting anywhere', of falling behind, being frozen out.

NR: At a less competitive, less frenetic pace, they might function well inside the limits imposed by their problems. But in New York all of their buttons start popping off. The thing they have fallen back on all of their life – their specialness – isn't getting them the recognition and rewards they want and a psychological explosion takes place. With so much of their energy focused on the competitiveness, they literally begin to fall apart.

CT: What kind of relationship do you develop with the client?

NR: Hopefully, an honest one. First and foremost, I want this individual to realize that the problems being brought to me do not make him or her an inferior person, a failure, someone who needs to be told what to do. Usually, new clients are emotionally exhausted. They need a place to at least regain strength and confidence. They need to feel welcome. And the first thing that happens is that they are terribly suspicious of me. Why not? They walk into a studio that has virtually no furniture, just rugs, cushions, a few small bookshelves, no pictures on the wall, nothing that resembles their idea of what psychotherapy is about. I don't wear a suit, probably haven't shaved for a few days and my clothes look like they were picked out by my mother twenty years ago. What is more, they have come for a session that will last from $1^{1}/_{2}$ to 2 hours and there is no fee. They will have to decide what to give me for my time and effort. Now this is so antithetical to what they are experiencing in New York, it is really unsettling. So initially, all of the suspicion is out – 'Who is this guy? What's the gimmick?'

CT: Why are you working this way rather than specifying what you need from a one hour or two hour session? What is your motive here?

NR: I have tried at various times to set a fee. There are many things I'd like to do for my wife and my former wife who is our partner in the retreat center we've opened upstate. I've spent many nights thinking about doing it but I simply cannot. Something inside changes when I think of charging; it becomes too much like commerce. I do a lot of work with my hands, using a form of healing touch. I don't want to feel as though I'm selling my hands to people in distress. If they are essentially free to determine what my services are worth to them and what they can afford – and this is by no means an easy balance to strike – then I don't feel as though I'm for sale; it frees me to just help them.

CT: The person faces a simplicity of setting, a certain informality in relationship and no request for a specific fee. What kind of responses come when people get exposed to all this?

NR: Despite their suspicion and fear, despite themselves, most open up. Something says to them, 'This is real.' And the part of themselves that has been waiting for this responds. That starts in motion another process: the fear that what they say about themselves will make me dislike them. So they begin speaking and at the same time try to hide, or at least clean up, the details. This is where the touching and meditation work is particularly effective, in breaking down that conditioned fear of the truth.

CT: So, there are these two forms of communication, one is the dialogue and the other is the laying on of the hands. Stress and tension lends itself to fear and paranoia. Do you have to establish trust in order to touch someone?

NR: People hear about me from their friends, co-workers, those they know and trust enough to try me out. That helps. But even so I might have to wait a while before I can touch someone very gently at the back of the neck and the crown of the head. It varies from person to person. I've been working with one individual for more than two years who still can't allow it. Being touched is incredibly difficult for many people. So I will spend a lot of time working only in relatively 'safe' areas like the back of the neck and the crown before I invite someone to lie down and learn about deep relaxation, how to find strength and comfort in the feeling of the ground, the freedom to be therapeutically touched.

CT: What is the purpose behind touching somebody?

NR: It involves a powerful transfer and infusion of energy. Not my energy but the natural energy around us being concentrated and directed through me into the person being touched. It is warm, reassuring and heartfelt. People who wouldn't speak about some troubled or difficult area of their life have the support inside at that point to begin. Suddenly their mind is sharper; the process of insight opens up and there is an ability to say aloud the hidden things that elsewhere might make you a pariah.

CT: The work of the hands allows a person to open up their heart to you. Do you find this a speedier vehicle than to just dialogue with a client?

NR: Absolutely. From a lifetime of talking, the client has built up a variety of dialogue defenses, verbal evasions. You can fence with them indefinitely and it's unnecessary. For example, one person from another part of the country did some very wonderful work with a therapist there before beginning with me. In describing the difference between his approach and mine, she said, 'You're both very similar but with you I get there faster.' Here is where I value speed. Without getting hooked on results, I do want to see my clients recover from their emotional wounds as quickly as they can and the use of touch facilitates that.

CT: What common kinds of suffering and significant changes come to mind?

NR: One of the most striking involved a woman who was convinced that she had been molested by her father. When she talked she would insist it had happened. But whenever she was on the ground, in a deep state, being touched gently on the head, heart, abdomen and back, the memories that returned to her were of a loving father playing with a small child; games that were affectionate but innocent. In that deep state, she loved him, delighted in his attention. This led to the discovery that her mother had interpreted their play as lewd, dirty. In ordinary conversation she superimposed her mother's viewpoint on her own, clear memories, obscuring them so much that she had cut herself off from her father. I remember the session in which it just 'dropped in'. She was in tears, thanking me for giving her back her father. And I was in tears, reminding her to call the therapist who had worked with her for years before me. Everybody should be in tears with this one. But neither he nor I returned her memories to her; it was this beautiful, powerful energy that touches the heart so deeply, gives us the courage to see through our confusion. However you are comfortable naming it – as universal life force, or as God – we are describing a presence of such magnitude that it can free us from our worst fears and delusions.

When I say to a client, 'Time to go to the ground, time to touch,' it is really an invitation to regain spirit, to feel this fully alive again.

CT: So clients gain liberating insights into past experiences. Would you say that working with their past is the primary thread of your work?

NR: Not really. In the example I just used, all the work done in relation to the woman's present circumstances wasn't mentioned. A good session is a finely-tuned balance of past and present. It can't be otherwise because the past is alive in everything we are doing right now. Without being incorporated in the present moment, an investigation of the past is merely an archaeological expedition, dead fact; however fascinating, it won't change what is happening today.

CT: Let us explore other kinds of clients and their personalities.

Drug addicts, prostitutes, criminals . . . what happens in these kinds of relationships? How do you deal with people living a nightmare existence?

NR: The first thing they have to feel from me is that it doesn't make a difference to me whether I'm talking to a druggie or a hooker or the president of the Chase Manhattan Bank. That I am not going to react to their lives according to a rule of law that sets them apart from the so-called 'good people'. The issue is not what they are doing but how they are going about it; whether or not they are living in harmony with their own desires and the consequences of their actions. In that respect it doesn't matter to me what people do. Once clients realize this, they have a much easier time talking to me, even without touch. It is a mistake to assume that the only nightmare existences are the socially unacceptable professions. Emotionality is just as addictive as drugs; depression is just as much of a chemical substance in this sense as heroin or cocaine. I know thieves I would trust with my life – and have. I am primarily interested in the quality of a person's behaviour, its essential nature, not the label it goes under. When I look at my own life, I can see my own grey areas, my own addictive behaviours, my own propensity to respond to appetite rather than reason. It is not difficult, for example, to find elements of prostitution in what I do. You come to Norm's studio and he loves you for a couple of hours and you leave some money on the way out. What does that sound like?

On Monday evenings I have a meditation class for all the people who do private sessions with me. It's beautiful to see them all sitting together, learning Vipassana (insight meditation), the touching work, becoming known to each other by how they work, not by the names they wear in society.

CT: I can't think of any psychotherapists who bring all the clients together for an evening's meditation.

NR: What they are learning in this aspect of the work is how to be themselves in front of others without shame or guilt. When I'm asked personal questions, I give as complete an answer as I can: they'll hear about the drugs, the army, all the wars beginning with growing up in the streets of Brooklyn. One person remarked in shock, 'How can you sit up there and tell such horrible stories about yourself?' Because they are true.

CT: What is the value for the client to hear about your experience. For example, psychoanalysts don't give a whisper of information about themselves. They regard themselves as being a blank sheet.

NR: That's artificial and unnatural. I never met a blank sheet I wanted to talk to.

CT: You are actually generating a lot of your personal history to the client. What *is* the value of doing that?

NR: We are in this together. I have had certain experiences that have moved me to discover certain things; I'm educated in the intricacies of the mind and the possibilities of the spirit. If you filter out this training and experience, there is not a whole lot of difference between me and my clients. On my own level, I must contend with my own problems, my own fears and hesitation. If they can't sense that I mean this, then I am just one more authority in their lives that they are forced by their pain to follow. Our work ceases to be an educating conversation, a moment of guidance, instruction from someone they trust.

CT: The woman asked: 'Norman, how can you tell such things about yourself?' There is evidently some surprise, if not shock, at what you say about yourself.

NR: But it is the truth. If I've done these things and learned something from them, the sense of shame about them can obviously be let go of, put to rest. But if I'm still ashamed of them, if I'm still ducking the truth about myself, then what can I possibly have to say about human behaviour that would be of value to others. Human beings, even the best of us, do some outrageous things in the course of our lives. That is not something to hide.

CT: It seems there is a mutual experience of sharing and opening up going on between yourself and the client.

NR: Very much so.

CT: One of the classical problems seems to be projection upon the therapist. Does that influence or effect that relationship in any way? Your personal history could increase the sense of awe and wonder – 'This guy has worked through so much.' Your history could accelerate the projection.

NR: This isn't just a matter of me talking about myself. The information has to be relevant to what the client is talking about. And it can't take over the conversation; it serves as a foundation that enables the client to continue, to reach a moment of understanding. It is instructional, not confessional. For example, if someone is unable to take their next step, I'll let them know where I am hesitating, let them see how I deal with that problem. Then we have a conversation starting about the 10,000 ways to deal with being stuck.

CT: What's the difference between the two of you?

NR: After all these years, I've finally learned how to move myself through the barriers that keep arising; they still haven't discovered that; they still need a guide.

CT: Concepts like 'energy' and 'God' can become abstract. So one really can't relate to them. Would you say your work is primarily psychotherapy, ie. working on unresolved emotional problems? Where does 'energy' or 'God' fit in?

NR: My work is whatever the person in front of me needs it to be. For some, a more verbal approach supported by the other practices is necessary; for others, we begin with more emphasis on meditation or on learning how to develop their communication with subtle energies. In all cases, the work stays rooted in specific experiences; it becomes what the person does, not an abstract.

CT: You have a number of resources available to you; hands, energy, meditation, communication.

NR: That's right. And within this range, I'll be whatever the person walking through the door needs me to be. This also changes from session to session; people seldom present only one continuous need.

CT: What happens if the person, over weeks or months, gives you the feeling that he or she is not really interested in deep fundamental change? You are a shoulder to cry on, someone to talk to who listens. What do you do in this circumstance?

NR: Call attention to it, quickly and very directly. That's easy for me. Subtlety in conversation isn't one of the things Brooklyn is famous for. I'll tell the person, 'Look, I have heard this twenty times and it's getting boring. You might be able to do this for the next three years but I'm not interested in that. Either you start moving or I stop listening.'

CT: What kind of response do you get?

NR: Most of the time, the person snaps out of it once the shock of being invited to leave wears off. Even if people don't have much experience with directness, they do seem to appreciate it. Once I was with a client who insisted on returning to old issues long resolved as a way of keeping the conversation safe. She was paying zero attention to what I was saying so finally I warned her that if she kept it up, I'd rather watch television. She ignored that too, so I turned on the set, watched a movie for about fifteen minutes. Then I asked her if she had had enough of this. She had. Seeing me turn away from her had sobered her up. We went back to work and she really began to talk. On another occasion, when I was working 70-75 hours a week, I told a client, 'Give me some help here. Make it interesting or you are going to loose me.' She looked at me and saw that I really was fading out. That woman did the best session she had done in months.

CT: The 'Idle Rich' come to see you because it is almost fashionable. Do the yuppies come to see you who simply want to feel comfortable with their lifestyle, their consumerism and obsession with making money?

NR: People who don't want to work, rich or poor, don't stay very long. I won't let them spin the litanies about themselves indefinitely and the meditation process also makes it difficult for them to indulge themselves. Stillness is a means for insight. Just experiencing the flow of the breath or the feeling of the ground creates room for impulses to surface that the person has been working very hard to buy beneath the consumerism. When that happens, the client either decides to face the issues or quits.

CT: A common conception of New York is that it is an environment of tension and hostility. Through touch, communication, meditation, their inner world is revealed through the release of emotional material. You are with this person for a two-hour period. Then they are back on the streets of New York, possibly quite vulnerable. Their defenses and resistances have dropped away. How does the person make the transition from an intense session with you back to being in Manhattan?

NR: With difficulty, but it is a part of the process. Being open does not mean only experiencing pleasantness; it involves a willingness to deal with whatever life offers at the moment. New York is a marvellous classroom for teaching that. If I see that somebody is too vulnerable, I might let them rest in the apartment and take my next client for a walk. I do a lot of sessions outdoors, by the river or in Central Park. It doesn't inhibit the touching work, either. In this city, nobody is alarmed by the sight of someone's head and neck being touched; I could be standing on the person's chest; as long as we weren't blocking traffic, no one would care.

CT: Isn't there the possibility of clients going through anxiety waiting to see you again the following week?

NR: Yes, but they know that they can always call me if things get difficult. I'll spend time on the phone with them; this softens the sense of separation.

CT: Isn't there the possibility that out of insight and appreciation clients will become dependent upon you. What is the process for completing their work with you?

NR: In the beginning, of course they become dependent. Their safety lies in the fact that I don't want them to remain tied to me by an inability to work on their own. This is not just a clinical situation, a place to fix broken personalities; it is an educational process, a matter of learning how to see into the process of life itself. I'll assign novels and poems where they highlight something a client needs to learn, do sessions in restaurants or in swimming pools; whatever is needed to get the point across and help the person integrate what we do and discuss into his or her daily life. This is where the meditation work and the subtle energy exercises are particularly valuable. You have to do them on you own; I can't sit and breathe for you.

CT: In the total process of the interaction between you and the client, signals come clear to you that the person is taking responsibility for their life. They also have more accessibility to meditation processes and energy.

NR: The shift is most noticeable in relation to everyday decisions that the client has to make. Instead of wanting me to make the decision, the person becomes more vocal, using me as a sounding board for his or her own ideas, or may even be telling me about decisions already made. At that point, the person is no longer being overwhelmed by problems; that's when the conversation really gets interesting. There are reasons then to continue working with me. They may develop a love of meditation and energy work and decide to study it more deeply as a subject independent of their problems; they may be ready to step beyond the body into other realms of existence. But now they are not compelled to stay with me; I become a real choice.

CT: How do you respond to clients whose lifestyle really contributes to their unhappiness?

NR: By making that the subject of our work right from the beginning. Recently, a young man from New York came to Devon to work with me on that very problem. At home he was working a seventy-hour week at a job he no longer enjoyed. Merely knowing the reasons why he was burying himself this way wasn't changing anything and after every session I would point this out to him, that nothing would be different until he made room in his schedule for it to be so – until he put down the drug, stopped overdosing on work. On retreat here, he began learning how to do that.

CT: Having made changes in their relationship to their activities, so there is balance and integration, what is the meditation going to do for them?

NR: Insight meditation enables them to see beyond their immediate circumstances into the very nature of themselves, the heart and soul of the unknown. They can begin examining more clearly their relationship to neighbours, community, nation and beyond this to the universe and the unknown which we approach through the reality of death.

CT: What you are describing is a movement for the client from a state of personal suffering and desperation to its transformation to the transcendent issues of life beyond personal circumstances.

NR: Yes, it's the blending of these two aspects of existence that enables us to complete our development as human beings. I know there is a lot of conversation about the difference between meditation and psychotherapy, but I have always looked upon them as complementary processes. You must deal with the issue of self in relation to the universe in which the self has been formed. Which aspect you begin with depends upon which tools you favour. I like the personal approach. I love working directly with people, being in the mud with them; and in the process helping them find the peace within that enables them to journey into the larger context.

CT: Even in New York?

NR: Especially in New York!

We must put aside our differences

An interview with Timothy Madden
Boston, Massachusetts, USA

The office of the AIDS Action Committee of Massachusetts is situated
on Boylston Street, Boston. I had made an appointment to meet with
Timothy Madden, an AIDS patient and counsellor, in one of the
rooms of the action group. It was lunchtime and the city office
workers were outside in the spring sunshine by the thousands. People
were heading for the parks, the restaurants, the buses and subways.
There was an air of heightened activity as people strolled and hurried
from one place to another.

I had to spend a few minutes in the upstairs waiting room. On the
coffee table in front of me was spread a wide range of literature on
AIDS, safe sex, drug abuse and the need to use a condom. There were
various photographs and illustrations in the literature to make the
point as explicit as possible about AIDS and the factors that contribute to an individual's infection by the virus.

The first leaflet I picked up, dated 1986, said: 'The Acquired
Immune Deficiency Syndrome or AIDS was first reported in the
United States in 1981. Since that time the Public Health Service has
received reports of more than 20,000 cases, about 54% of which have
resulted in death. An estimated 1.5 million people (in the US) have
been infected by the virus that causes AIDS but have no symptoms of
illness.'

The leaflet goes on to say that infection with the virus which is
referred to as HIV (Human Immunodeficiency Virus) does not always
lead to AIDS. 'Most individuals infected with HIV have no symptoms
and feel well. Some develop symptoms which may include tiredness,
fever, loss of appetite and weight, diarrhea, night sweats and swollen
glands.

'The time between infection with HIV virus and the onset of
symptoms (the incubation period) ranges from about six months to
five years or more. Not everyone exposed to the virus develops AIDS.

'AIDS cases have been reported from all 50 states [in the US] and
more than a hundred other countries. Cases continue to increase in
cities and towns throughout the US. Currently there are no antiviral
drugs available anywhere that have been proven to cure AIDS.'

Timothy arrived punctually and the two of us went to a room to sit and talk together. The form of the interview is basically a chronological account of the flow of his life in recent years. The Vietnam war, alcohol addiction, being HIV positive and then contracting AIDS have not made life an easy road for Timothy. Yet, in spite of all this, Timothy has sustained commitment to working with the facts of his life and his relationship to those facts.

But it is necessary to point out here that Timothy, as a gay man in his mid-30's, is blessed with an invaluable dual support system. One is the AIDS Action Committee where he works as a volunteer on the hotline. The second is the gay community itself, which has rallied together to an extraordinary degree as the day-to-day AIDS crisis continues into what may be a long term future. By and large homosexuals and bisexuals, who make up 65% of AIDS cases in the US, know that they are in a high risk category. The result of this is that gays are giving support to each other to deal with the threat to their personal lives and their community. But, of course, many sufferers, including gays, still experience rejection from friends, family and society.

The users of intravenous drugs (17% of all AIDS cases) often do not experience any real support. They mostly live in a lonely world alienated from others with the fear and secrecy of being a drug user. So when they find out they are infected with the AIDS virus their alienation and terror is intensified.

As I sat and talked with Timothy, it became apparent to me from the onset that I was talking with an unusually clear-minded and articulate person who had worked hard on himself over the years. His answers to my questions during the course of an hour-long meeting came over with that quiet authority of a man in touch with himself.

CT: Would you tell me about your background before you knew you were carrying the AIDS virus?

TM: I was born in New York City and I studied in parochial schools there. I had a fairly normal childhood, then went into the armed service when I was twenty and spent a year in Vietnam. When I came back, I started working, met someone and moved to the Boston area where I was trained as a respiratory therapist and started working at a large Boston hospital. In 1984 I was diagnosed with pulmonary tuberculosis and began treatment for that. Either the treatment was unsuccessful or I was very slow to respond to it, so it was thought that I might be carrying the AIDS virus.

As treatment for my tuberculosis I had been receiving injections. In 1985, I was involved in a needle stick accident that brought about the need for me to take the AIDS test. The nurse gave me an injection and when she was putting the cap back on the needle, she stuck her finger. One of the major ways that the AIDS virus can be transmitted is by the use of needles so we were concerned. I sat down with my physician and the nurse and we decided that I would test for HIV antibody. I tested positive.

I had known about the test before and had been counselled about the pros and cons of taking it. However, I decided up to that point that I didn't want to have the test. But in this case I felt it was necessary.

CT: What were the pros and cons for you? I would think that the pros would be dominant.

TM: I consulted with my primary physician and it was his opinion that the test was available for me if I chose to take it. I also spoke to people here in the AIDS Action Committee who are involved in education and their concern was, what would I do with the information, whether positive or negative, when I got it? If I was positive how would it affect my life and my psyche? All it meant to me was that if I was positive I would continue doing things that I was already doing. I would live my life within safe and rational guidelines and stay as healthy as possible. If I tested negative I would also be doing the exact same thing. So there didn't seem to be any sense in taking the test – until my decision affected the nurse, who also happened to be considering having a child at this time.

CT: From the time you decided to take the test to the time of getting the result, what was that period like for you?

TM: One word. Anxiety. I had been waiting four weeks. It took longer than usual because they did two tests. The first came positive and just to make sure that it was not a false positive they did another test. On one of my routine visits my physician called me into his office and we talked about it. I had developed a close friendship with him when I worked with him as a respiratory therapist, before any of this began.

CT: When the doctor said that you were HIV positive, what did you feel?

TM: Well, actually, when he told me, the anxiety seemed to wane. I knew testing positive was a distinct possibility from the way that I had chosen to live as a gay man. Knowing the different risk categories, I was somewhat convinced that I would be positive. There was this little part of me that said maybe it won't be, maybe I'll slip through somehow. In fact, there was some relief in knowing where I stood. I was 35 years old at the time.

CT: What were the next steps for you?

TM: I thought of who I might tell. I do have a life partner, so the most important thing was to tell him. The test result was not a surprise. He knew I was being tested because of the needle stick accident. We had talked about the situation previously and we agreed that the chances were that I would come up positive. I guess the greatest stress was in wondering whether we should both be tested. But that's not the route we chose. We are very close and we had pledged to stick by each other, no matter what the results were, no matter what might happen.

CT: That shows quite a degree of commitment from both of you.

TM: Yes it does. My major concern with telling other people was the confidentiality issue. Now that I was in the category of HIV positive, what would that mean for the work place, in regard to insurance and benefits and all of that? And, of course, of paramount consideration was how do I treat this medically? What can I do now that I know I'm positive? How is this affecting the tuberculosis? My response was to educate myself: reading scientific journals, communicating more with my physician, getting specialists that he knew to give me more information on what the possibilities were, attending every seminar and health conference including alternative therapies conferences, and to find out what was available through the AIDS Action Committee. I wanted to get as much knowledge about my situation as I could.

CT: Would you say that if somebody knows that they are HIV positive, it's useful and important for that person to go out and be well informed?

TM: Absolutely.

CT: Isn't there some risk that in acquiring so much knowledge, it can actually intensify the anxieties and fears?

TM: Oh, I don't think so. I think that if the information is presented properly by responsible people, there is no harm. Going to seminars and workshops made me feel that I wasn't alone in this. I was not isolated; there were other people at the workshops that I could talk to. They shared how they felt about their situation and how they reacted. There was a strength in numbers. We were all going through this together and I was not alone. I've heard that 1.5 million are already HIV positive.

Recently there was an article in the *New York Times* saying the AIDS health crisis will, most likely, be a major political issue. AIDS is not as abstract to people as the politics of the Middle East or South Africa. AIDS is right here. It's right in the hospital when I go for my injections. It's right down the block. It's in my church. Politics and morality are conflicting. There is the moral agenda interfering with a major catastrophic health issue and that will have to be ironed out in the elections. This will reach a pinnacle.

CT:　You told your life partner. What decisions did you make about communicating with parents, brothers, sisters, employers and close friends who may not be so understanding?

TM:　I only informed the closest of friends. I felt no other necessity, with the exception of health care providers that may be drawing my blood, oor a dentist. Those situations didn't actually arise but they are examples. In fact, a situation did happen where a lab technician was going to draw some blood and she didn't have on gloves. I told her that I had blood precautions and let her take it from there. Otherwise I didn't feel it was necessary to be advertising or telling everyone.

CT:　In other words, you used your discretion with regard to whom you actually informed. Has there been any kind of backlash or difficult situations for you because you are HIV positive?

TM:　I didn't feel any discrimination or backlash. Later on when I got the AIDS diagnosis that changed a little bit. But at that point, no, I felt nothing. Things went on quite as much as they had normally. I was pleased that I had another piece of information to add to the puzzle about my health and the tuberculosis. But basically life went on as usual with the exception that I knew that I had been infected with the virus and that there were possibilities down the road of getting AIDS. I knew I should do all that was possible to optimize my situation.

CT:　Were you also making changes in your diet and taking exercise, as well as increasing your knowledge?

TM:　After getting the knowledge I could have just sat there, with all the information and do nothing – sit in an easy chair, watch cartoons and drink beer. But when I got more information I had to put it into effect. My diet changed; I exercised; I looked into some of the holistic therapies, meditation and other approaches.

CT: How much time passed between being diagnosed as HIV positive and being diagnosed with AIDS?

TM: One year and two months. In November 1986, a major change took place. I could no longer use the bicycle at the gym as long as I was used to. I was getting a little short of breath. The apartment I live in is up a long flight of stairs and I noticed that I had to stop half way up the stairs to rest. On a visit to my pulmonary physician I mentioned this to him and he sent me to X-ray which turned out to be normal. Prophylactically he started me on an antibiotic for pneumonia, a general broad-based antibiotic. Three to four days later there was an improvement. When he took another chest film there were bilateral infiltrates on the entire lung. He admitted me and performed a bronchoscopy.

CT: What is that?

TM: During a bronchoscopy a tube is placed through the mouth or nose into the lung and then a culture is taken of the tissues and secretions that are in the lung. He admitted me to the hospital and the next day the results were back. The cultures that he got were positive for a numercistic pneumonia. I was started on bacterum. He and my psychiatrist, who I had been seeing for two years on a weekly basis, came into my room and told me what I already knew. I had felt certain that I had AIDS and hearing the diagnosis gave me a sense of relief. Sometimes I'm misunderstood when I say that in support groups, since they have difficulty understanding why I felt a sense of relief.

CT: Why did you feel relieved?

TM: I had been in battle for three years with TB and I had known for more than a year that I was HIV positive. Since I wasn't responding to the treatment for TB, I was confused and uncertain about what was going on. I didn't know whether I had a rare form of TB, or a particular type of pneumonia, or if I had AIDS. Now I knew what it was and so, at first, where many feel panic when they hear for the first time, for me there was a feeling of relief. Now I knew exactly what I was dealing with . . . That feeling didn't last too long.

CT: After you were told that you had AIDS, you had to then go back home and tell your partner.

TM: He came to the hospital. We all knew what it means when an HIV positive gay man in his mid-30s comes down with pneumonia.

That rings a bell for everyone I know in the circles that I travel in. So when I called him and I said, 'I think you better come in and talk,' he said, 'It's it.' And I said, 'It's it.' So we were quite well-prepared. Some people aren't and there are many different stories. I don't want mine to sound like the norm.

CT: It seems from what you say that you have had unusually supportive people with you – your partner as well as your psychiatrist, doctor and the AIDS Action Committee.

TM: Oh, absolutely.

CT: What changes has AIDS made to your personal relationship?

TM: He has taken on an extra caring, and he tolerates more. I think I get away with a little more. (*Laughter*).

CT: In the beginning, how much of your daily life was dominated by the knowledge of carrying AIDS, in terms of thoughts and perceptions? Did you find yourself putting the facts aside?

TM: When I got out of the hospital in the beginning of December I dove right into Christmas shopping as an escape. I did nothing but shop all day and avoid thinking about it. I just took whatever medications I had to take. I went to concerts, shows, and I didn't think very much. Then on January 1st I started on the drug AZT which I had to take every four hours. Taking this medication became a reminder of my condition. Every four hours of every single day, including 4 a.m. when I wake from my sleep to take these pills, reminds me that I have AIDS. It is an issue that I am still working on with my psychiatrist. The little box that I take out of my pocket that is always with me says, 'You have AIDS,' every time I take a pill! Hopefully they will come up with something where I'll only have to do it once a day. That simple thing like taking my medicine had a very strong effect when I first started it in January.

CT: Three or four months have gone by. How has the adjustment been? Are you still taking the medicine with such frequency?

TM: Yes. I'm not a very good house guest when the alarm goes off at 4 a.m.

CT: What about work and financial support?

TM: I worked for the Boston University Medical Centre. In April 1984, I was placed on Workman's Compensation for TB. Some people get the disease and are treated and it's taken care of very quickly. I have been on a fixed income since then, living at a salary range of the 1984 level. At times it's been difficult and I've accrued some bills on the way. Yesterday I filed for bankruptcy in the Federal Court so I cleared the books. Hereon in I have the basic type of financial commitments. All of the other stuff is cleared out of the way.

CT: What is your relationship to daily life and living one day at a time?

TM: Living one day at a time . . . That's the phrase that does the trick for me. Living one day at a time. I hate to take the credit or brag but I'm a little better at it than say some members of my support group. For seven years I've been a member of Alcoholics Anonymous. After Vietnam I had a problem with alcohol and substance abuse. I haven't had beverage alcohol in seven years. I did it basically through the philosophy of AA – taking it one day at a time. So I carried a lot of that into my next disease. From alcoholism to tuberculosis to AIDS. Each one is like a battle, a big war. I've seen more friends go with AIDS than I ever saw friends go in Vietnam.

CT: That's a strong statement. How are you relating to each other in the AIDS community?

TM: We give each other strength. It's amazing how we can put our differences aside when this happens. In my support group when there is a little X between us, that is so background, so secondary. We just put that aside and help each other, be there for each other and love each other. Social bonding takes place, too. People get together to go out after groups or share little projects together. There is a group of men in my support group who are renting a cottage for the summer by the ocean to be together and be supportive of each other. All sorts of bonding goes on within the group. We talk about our advocates and what they are going for us and what they are not doing.

CT: Mutual support is obviously invaluable.

TM: I don't think any of us would be doing quite as well as we have been without each other. We all get a chance to check in on where we are and lend support to others who may be sicker or we just share our experiences of how we dealt with telling our mother, or the problems we are having with our landlord or landlady.

We are also supported by the AIDS Action Committee. They have a pastoral concerns sub-committee which represents, as far as I'm concerned, all religions and all major denominations. Recently I attended a retreat at a Franciscan monastery with ten people with AIDS and four people from the pastoral concerns committee. It was uplifting and wonderful even though it's not the established church that I grew up with. The committee is doing a fabulous job and there is a spiritual element there which is rekindling me.

CT: With all the risk to life, there emerges love, friendship, empathy and support.

TM: And hope. For me it is becoming evident that I am being transformed by AIDS. I'm seeing aspects of my own spirituality that I've never seen before. It's transforming me with regard to my relationship to other human beings. And, most important, it's transforming me towards a new understanding of what we are as inhabitants on this planet. This disease is not in this one little corner nor is it one problem for one little sub-group. This is a planetary problem and all humanity is affected by it. I can put difficulties aside in my support group, and as inhabitants on this planet we will have to put our differences aside to deal with this as brothers and sisters together. There is a great transformation taking place in my life through this and it continues one day at a time.

After the meeting, Timothy and I walked out into the April sunshine and joined the flow of office workers. At the traffic lights, we hugged and parted company.

INQUIRY

What is our attitude?

An interview with Vimalo Kulbarz
Totnes, England

Vimalo Kulbarz, who is from West Germany, has an identical twin
brother. In the mid-1950s when both were in their teens, they decided
that they wanted to become Buddhist monks. At this time there were
very few books on Buddhism and what was available was generally a
translation of the countless sutras (talks) of the Buddha. There were
barely any western Buddhist monks in the world.

Vimalo travelled to London and in 1958 took ordination. He
shaved his head, put on the saffron robes, and undertook to observe
the widespread disciplines. After two years he flew to Burma.

Vimalo (the name means 'without blemish') continued to live in
Burma and spent years engaged in intensive meditation under the
instruction of the late Mahasi Sayadaw, probably the most venerated
meditation teacher in Burma this century. Few teachers in the Buddhist tradition have earned themselves such a formidable reputation as
Mahasi Sayadaw. He demanded from his students an unparalleled
degree of mindfulness; not even the arm was to be moved without
giving total attention to the changing experience of it. The practice
contributed to determining the simple actualities of human experience from the fantasies, daydreams, memories and planning. The
state of consciousness was not the same after participating in such a
disciplined process.

As the years went by, Vimalo became increasingly interested in
western psychology's insights into the mind-body process, the Buddhist texts in Pali and Sanskrit, as well as the texts which were
translated, and the inter-connectedness of the religious experience.

From Burma Vimalo moved to take up residence in a remote region
in south-west Thailand called Gaby. In order to meet with him, you
had to walk through a huge natural arch and into a large valley,
virtually unspoiled. The valley was the home for all manner of wild
creatures, including monkeys, scorpions, cobras, tropical birds and
many rodents. Here Vimalo built himself a kuti (a hut) on legs, with a
large window in order that he could look down the valley. He has
spent years in virtual solitude.

Once while on a country bus, Vimalo had a religious experience which enabled him to perceive the essence of the spiritual life. One of the outcomes of this was a lengthy article with more than three hundred notations which he wrote called 'Awakening to the Truth'. It showed the universality of such an experience.

I would visit him every few months for a few days during the early seventies to talk with him about my meditation experience, my attitudes and the deeper meaning of what was being communicated in the Buddhist sutras. The meetings were never easy, although invaluable. He simply refuses to allow one to waffle. He questions directly when one is using concepts without really understanding what they mean. He does not think it useful to talk about what one has not experienced.

He has this ability to recognise immediately where somebody is clinging blindly to a view or opinion or attached to some particular way of seeing either themselves, others or religious practices. He regards the willingness to point things out to another as an expression of genuine friendship.

In 1976 Vimalo returned to West Germany where he became the resident teacher at the Haus der Stille (House of Silence), a meditation centre in Rosenburg, near Hamburg. In recent years he devised and authored a spiritual board game called 'Challenges – A Game of Self Discovery'. He has taught insight meditation retreats in different parts of the world. In the early 1980s he disrobed after twenty-five years as a Buddhist monk.

In the interview, we investigate feelings, attitudes and self-acceptance.

CT: I would like to explore the possible benefits which are available to an individual who wishes to learn about himself or herself. In what way do meditation and psychotherapy contribute to the welfare of the individual? What are the similarities and the dissimilarities?

VK: Both emphasise knowing oneself. In psychotherapy this is frequently an analytical process. In insight meditation it can develop gradually into a holistic awareness through getting in touch with the essential nature of the mind which is pure awareness.

CT: One may have a genuine interest to observe and so know oneself in daily life, including activities and conversation, but it may not be happening. What prevents this?

VK: Many people in the West have difficulties accepting themselves. They often have such a deep-rooted feeling of hopelessness that they are convinced that they cannot change their predicament. This would prevent a person from further examination. Often one is led into an unresolved problem by unpleasant feelings. But if I don't like unpleasant feelings, I don't pay close attention to them and therefore I don't examine what is behind the unpleasant feeling. Or if I think the problem is in other people or situations then I am not examining what this situation is telling me about myself or about what I could learn or practise in this situation.

CT: Is this an analytical process?

VK: At first, this examination is somewhat analytical but if one pursues it then the intuitive faculty is developed so that one is able to see immediately what is really going on. Right Understanding, the first aspect of the Buddha's Eightfold Path, is the ability to see intuitively the totality of a given situation.

CT: The problem which appears is born from contact with various kinds of inner feelings, but the person finds the same feelings keep coming up again and again. They are not being resolved despite the effort to give attention to the feelings and what is lying behind them. The person's mind is still troubled.

VK: Any unresolved problem we have comes up again and again because its energy is not yet exhausted. If I am aware of this I might approach the problem with a different attitude by experimenting with my way of handling it. The important thing is not so much whether my problem comes up again and again but my attitude and approach to it. People who find it difficult to accept themselves regard any problem as a proof of their worthlessness. This sets off a vicious circle of negative qualities: doubts about oneself, inferiority feelings, depression. Therefore, one is more and more incapable of handling any situation adequately. One needs not only Right Understanding but also the second aspect of the Eightfold Path, namely Right Attitude, which includes faith and patience. If one has patience it does not really matter how often the same problem turns up. And yet, people who can't accept themselves have little or no faith.

CT: Some people who reject themselves can emerge with a very strong religious faith. People who are suicidal suddenly find a religion. Others who lack or who have lost their spiritual direction suddenly find a guru.

VK: Human beings go into psychology or turn to religion for the simple reason that they are suffering. People who find it difficult to accept themselves often uphold a very high idealism which further aggravates their problem. For example, religious precepts, when they are handled without wisdom and discernment, can often enhance this problem of not accepting oneself because one is comparing oneself all the time with exalted beings instead of dealing directly with one's own problems and difficulties.

CT: Let's say a person has come to a deeper acceptance of himself or herself and is largely free of the tendency to undermine oneself. What next? Does one pursue further psychological understanding or spiritual development – if they can be distinguished from each other?

VK: That depends very much on what one considers to be the goal and purpose of one's life. Is it to be relatively free from conflicts or is the freedom from conflicts and emotional upheavals a necessary stage in one's spiritual evolution? Steadiness of mind and purpose is one of the indispensable prerequisites for going more deeply into the meditation. And profound stillness is necessary for deeper spiritual experiences culminating in enlightenment.

CT: The Buddha has referred frequently to the importance of the heart: love, compassion, spiritual joy and peace. Is there a direct connection between inquiry, the willingness to learn and these qualities of the heart? Is love a natural outflow of the willingness to learn from life?

VK: It again depends on one's attitude, approach, level of consciousness and purpose in life. Is it the willingness to learn more about dealing with outward things, adjusting to society and fitting into it; or is it more in the direction of inner transformation? In order for someone to experience spiritual joy and peace, one of the indispensable preconditions is considerable experience in meditation. Love and compassion presupposes that one can accept oneself. These four qualities you mentioned presuppose considerable spiritual maturity. If through meditation the mind becomes really tranquil, these qualities may manifest themselves spontaneously without any thought or direct effort of bringing them about. That is why meditation is of such great importance on the spiritual path.

CT: You say that as self-acceptance becomes present in one's life there emerges out of that a genuine love for others and some kind of faith. A faith in what?

VK: It is a deep conviction that whatever happens to us has meaning. Such a faith is strengthened by applying the principles of the spiritual life in one's daily life, especially if that is showing some effect in transforming one's life. To me, a meaningful life is to understand more and more what life is telling us all the time; a meaningful life is a life which is dedicated to inner growth. Out of that there arises a deep faith that we are living in a meaningful universe.

CT: Religion has attempted to give ultimate meaning to life. People are constantly told to 'have faith'.

VK: The different founders of religion had a direct insight into the meaning of life. Genuinely religious people don't have that problem of thinking that life has no meaning for them. I think that so many troubles of the present time stem from the fact that for a considerable number of people life has no meaning. Since many of us cannot accept the traditional values, we have to find out for ourselves what is the purpose and meaning of life. And that is far more arduous than accepting the values of a particular religion from our parents or the society we live in.

CT: Is this the search for meaning?

VK: The search for meaning is important. Besides giving meaning to one's life in general we can also discover the meaning of whatever happens to us. All the time life presents us with the opportunity for inner growth and development. Whatever happens to us is often a mirror of our own mind and attitudes. It is a question of whether we use these opportunities and become aware of how all things are interrelated; or whether we just drift along and have a good time, whatever that may mean. I believe if we continue with meditation and the inquiry and are not getting stuck with any form of achievement then our life becomes more and more meaningful. We are also preparing the ground, so to say, for enlightenment, that sudden breakthrough into the unconditioned. I feel that enlightenment is the ultimate goal of human existence and also the ultimate fulfilment.

CT: You are saying that there is an activity that human beings can participate in during their life journey which is both spiritual and psychotherapeutic, culminating in enlightenment.

VK: In the teaching of the Buddha we find a very subtle and comprehensive form of spiritual psychology which includes all the vast ranges of mind, not only the so-called shadow but also the almost limitless potential of the mind. I don't see why one should make a distinction between the spiritual and psychotherapeutic approach. To me the essence of the spiritual life is freedom.

By examining myself, my reactions, feelings, thoughts and attitudes and by learning to handle the challenges of life more adequately and creatively there is more freedom. Though enlightenment gives the ultimate freedom, there are so many areas where we can work in the direction of greater inner freedom: freedom from conventions, from fear, from opinions and from conditioning. This process of freeing oneself from conditioning is a spiritual and psychotherapeutic process. Many of us have a certain tendency to think in terms of 'either-or' instead of 'as well as'.

CT: With religion there is frequently the desire for security. Sometimes one is for the expression of one religion and against another. Involvement in psychotherapy can also became an end in itself rather than a tool.

VK: In all human beings the desire for security is fairly strong. In religion this desire finds a fertile breeding ground. That is why awareness and self-knowledge are so very important on the spiritual path, otherwise the danger is that one gets stuck because one feels secure. The Buddha used the Parable of the Raft to describe our life situation. He said it is as if a man is on a long journey and comes to a wide river and sees there is no way of getting across. So out of the branches and wood which he finds near the shore he builds himself a raft and with the help of the raft he crosses over to the other shore. The Buddha asked the monks whether it would be wise for that man to carry the raft out of gratitude because it had been so helpful to him. Obviously the monks said the man should abandon the raft.

CT: In what ways do we cling to the raft?

VK: The profound significance of the Parable of the Raft shows to me that all our attainment and achievements have significance only for the time being, but we should not get attached to them and cling to them. By letting them go we approach the next challenge anew. Many people on the spiritual path seem to consider the Way as an accumulation of positive qualities. They don't seem to see that whatever is helpful on one level of one's spiritual practice might be quite inadequate on the next level and it might even block one's further progress. Faith shows a profound and adequate solution coming out of the depth of one's being. In learning to meet the challenges of life in a creative way, one has to let go of the solutions of the past and ask oneself, 'What is the adequate way of handling this situation irrespective of the way that I handled this situation before?' The past gives us a certain feeling of security but whenever I feel too secure there is the danger of stagnation.

CT: One of the dangers of working on oneself is that there can come about a certain preoccupation with oneself and a forgetfulness of the world of suffering outside of oneself. That is a charge levelled at Buddhism as well as at psychotherapy.

VK: I think it is important to realise that in every situation in life there is on the one hand the possibility of growth and on the other hand there is a certain danger of one-sidedness, of attachment, of activating some kind of negative tendencies, or of using that situation to strengthen the ego. The Buddha said the highest kind of person is he or she who is concerned with both his or her well-being but is also concerned about the well-being of others. I don't think it necessarily follows if one is concerned about one's own growth that one does not bother any more about others. On the other hand, one can often see that the concern with others is frequently an escape from oneself. Unless there is clarity in myself and in the handling of my life I feel I'm in no position to help others. The same is with peace. I feel an essential aspect of peace is to be at peace with myself, learning to integrate the so-called shadow. Another important aspect is to bring peace into the relationships I have with other people, especially those I live with. An essential element of a peaceful way of life is to learn to handle conflicts.

CT: Some of the criticism levelled at Buddhism and psychotherapy is that there are seemingly too few people who take conflicts from the microcosm and look at the macrocosm of the same basic conflicts.

VK: I know quite a few people on the spiritual path who are seriously concerned with applying the principles of the spiritual practice to their daily life and their dealings with other people and have noticed a considerable change taking place. I don't think that one could say of such people that they are not concerned with 'the world of suffering outside of themselves'.

CT: There is probably never going to be a time when there is perfect clarity and order within. Are you saying that one must concentrate totally on oneself and on one's individual situation through watching oneself prior to active participation in the world of events?

VK: What is more important is a person's inner attitude towards whatever he or she is doing and his or her awareness and insight into the situation. Some people withdraw into themselves because they are unable to deal with other people or situations adequately. Others can't stay with themselves and become busy with other people.

CT: Sometimes a person starts off with a reasonably clear attitude but gradually the ego beings to get involved and the situation is used to boost the ego.

VK: Awareness and self-knowledge are indispensable on the spiritual path especially when we are living at a time when there is a re-evaluation of all values. Without awareness and self-knowledge one easily deceives oneself and uses things, activities or qualities of heart and mind to boost the ego, or we get stuck because we feel secure. What one needs in such a situation more than anything else is some genuine friends who do not hesitate to point things out. Very often we feel that something has gone wrong with our life but can't see a solution. Then we start doing something in order to stifle the feeling of discontent. But if we are not aware of the real nature and significance of this discontent we might become increasingly more busy and go further astray from finding a solution. We get more and more active but we are no longer in touch with ourselves. In such a situation a friend can be a very good mirror.

CT: Your words remind me of a statement of the Buddha. He said that a good friend is not one who flatters but one who actually points things out to another. The trouble is that sometimes we resist if things are pointed out to us. Our defences come in.

VK: If we find it difficult to accept ourselves, criticism triggers off old pain and defensive patterns. So we tend to reject the criticism, irrespective of whether it is true or not. But if I see that this reaction only increases the problem I might adopt a completely different attitude to criticism and allow myself to be more vulnerable. Can I examine whether there is something to the criticism? If I say something to another is it coming out of an attitude of love and compassion? Do I want the person to grow?

CT: In that respect, spirituality is not just concerned with self-preoccupation. Inner and outer perceptions are inseparable from each other.

VK: I feel the challenge of our time is not to escape from the world but to see an opportunity for inner growth and spiritual practice in all the challenges of life. That demands an enormous flexibility and 'skill in means'. It is skill of means to handle the different situations appropriately. Very often, when we want a particular method, we want to be certain of results.

CT: The challenge of actual life situations makes other challenges such as success and reaching the top seem somewhat minor.

VK: Many people on the spiritual path either accept the values of society – success, power, profit – or reject them and drop out. The middle path seems to me to examine the values of our present day society and understand our attitude to them, and then find out what is our own purpose in life and how we are living our life. Are we happy? Do we live a meaningful life? Are we growing inwardly? Is there an inner transformation? Are we helping others to grow?

CT: These are challenging questions. Thank you, Vimalo.

From the known to the unknown

An interview with Sister Kathleen England
Rome, Italy

Sister Kathleen England was born and brought up in England. She is rather cagey about revealing how old she is. In fact, she adamantly refuses to tell. I found it rather amusing. One tends to have this image that nuns who have dedicated their life to God and service are rather unconcerned about such worldly things as age and appearance. It seemed to me that in the case of Sister Kathleen she still retained that perception of herself as a human being, woman and nun. That seemed to me to be very healthy. One of her Italian friends told me that whenever she has to visit her convent in Wimbledon, London, she chooses to take the 27-hour train journey from Rome in order to honour her vow of poverty. She saves little in terms of a chartered air flight. No easy trip for an ordained senior citizen who adds to her discomfort by refusing to take a sleeping berth.

During the 1930s Sister Kathleen realized that she had a vocation for the contemplative life. So she decided, with that quiet dedication that characterizes her personality, to go to a Carmelite convent in Chichester, Sussex, often regarded by Roman Catholics as one of the most severe of the religious contemplative regimes. Her heart's wish was to take up the life 'behind the grill'. After undergoing a trial period, the Mother Superior and sisters in the convent decided not to let her stay. They recognized her vocation but advised her to enter into an active order. Sister Kathleen told me, 'I came out weeping and wailing.'

She took their advice and somewhat reluctantly, it seems, joined the Ursuline Order which is a teaching order with schools all around the world. In the late 1930s she was sent to Rome and fascist Italy when the jack-boot mentality and Mussolini ('I shall turn the Mediterranean into an Italian lake') were at their political height.

From there she was sent to the Caribbean as a teaching sister. To her satisfaction she found that being a member of the Ursuline Order fulfilled two needs, the contemplative and the active. Part of her commitment to the order was to give three hours a day to meditation as well as recite the daily office of prayer and reflection. Sister Kathleen also spent years in the Far East, especially the Philippines.

Nuns take the three vows of poverty, chastity and obedience. And it is often the last one which presents one of the great challenges to the ordained nun. Her superiors decide when and for how long a member of the order is based in a particular place. Though a nun may express a great deal of dissatisfaction, if not pain, with being located in a particular part of the world, she cannot simply get a new posting.

Sister Kathleen told me how much she appreciated her years in the East. She had her first exposure there to other religious contemplative traditions. On one visit to India, she remembered how she learnt that some of the sisters in a teaching order had never, in fact, visited the nearby Hindu temple nor had made any efforts to find out about the religious beliefs and practices of the local people living near their convent and schools.

In the 1970s she returned to Rome to live with the order there. Her whole life had been spent living in community. After requests and with some degree of patience, the superiors of the order gave her permission to move out of the convent and into a little bedsitter in the centre of the city. It was the first time in her life that she had to support herself financially, as well as cook, shop and work outside of her teaching role. She now spends her days meeting people, making a contribution to inter-faith understanding and translating religious books from Italian into English. She has worked for several years for the Vatican Council for Interreligious Dialogue.

In 1984 she was introduced to Professor Corrado Pensa, who teaches Eastern religions and philosophy at Rome University. She was introduced to his mediation classes and dharma group, which he leads in the heart of the city. The meetings became a catalyst for inter-religious dialogue at the experiential level. Sister Kathleen told me recently (1990), 'My aim is to devote as much time as the Lord gives me to developing a great deal more on the subject of Christian/Buddhist contemplation.'

I met Sister Kathleen in the apartment of a friend, Francesca Rusciani, in Rome.

CT: What do you mean by 'contemplation?'

Sr: It's a word that is quite difficult and quite popular. It's even a catch word and has all sorts of levels. I think it represents something that we are all looking for. The derivation of the word is 'to look'. Contemplation is the highest form of what we can try for in this life, as long as we see it includes everything.

CT: If contemplation means to look and to keep looking then what is worth looking for? What is worth contemplating? You say, 'Look at everything.' What would that mean for someone?

Sr: There is an ancient Christian writer who talks about looking at the reasons behind things or looking at the 'inner flame of things'. It's connected with one's faith and gives context to the attitude of looking.

For example, lately I have been looking at nature. I can look at a tree that has produced new leaves and flowers in total silence and stillness. I attempt to contemplate in the way I see it. When I look in this way, I see the reasons behind things, as the ancient writer says. Those reasons are connected in my mind with a power and energy that comes from somewhere else. As a Christian, I name this energy God who is the creator. I see this going through everything. This is called the first contemplation, the natural contemplation, which I reach by practice.

CT: So contemplation here means to take something in nature, like a tree, and totally look at it. Then I begin to see more than just what I am immediately confronted with, namely the form, colour and shape of the tree.

Sr: But I would distinguish something here. An artist would simply see the colour, form and shape of the tree. The scientist sees the cells. The ecologist looks at the tree with a feeling that it could be harmed. I would look at it in connection with the energies of God, himself. The Spirit is then working.

CT: So because of its energy, the tree becomes a manifestation, an intimation of something transcendent to it. And that spirit in looking makes it contemplative.

Sr: I think so. This is very sketchy and unfinished. I used a tree as an example because I was looking at a tree as I was sitting here. But I think as you go on with the practice of contemplation, it doesn't matter what you look at. You come to feel something greater than yourself.

CT: Does one need to take something from the visible world or can one also look within?

Sr: You can look into yourself and you may have no object there. But you are still contemplating. With an attitude of awareness, my 'original nature', shall we say, is what I am contemplating. For me contemplation is always connected with something bigger than myself. I don't think you necessarily need an object to know something greater. As you begin to enter into a contemplative way, you may need an object, as a kind of mediation to help you along. Then you may reach the attitude in which you're in a state of awareness of being. Now how it takes you through to something else greater I think is a question of faith. It is this faith which tells you something. When you reach that point of contemplation you are going beyond the natural contemplation to reach the transcendent which is beyond you. By faith you know the transcendent is there.

CT: What would be an example of natural faith.

Sr: According to my understanding, faith which is basic to contemplation is something which I receive as a gift and I think all on this earth receive. Faith is given to us because God has enlightened all who come into this world. Enlightenment is a word of scripture which I believe in very much. Enlightening is another word for faith.

CT: Are you saying faith is a gift which all human beings receive by virtue of being human? In a state of inward contemplation, this gift is present and doesn't have to be looked for or developed.

Sr: I think faith is there with the contemplation and develops in power and capacity in a natural way. It comes to another level when it is connected with scriptural revelation, which gives more details about what the scripture signifies. But as far as faith goes, the definition of faith itself is to have the certainty of something which you cannot perceive. So there you have something mysterious but still an existing reality. In the Bible, faith, hope and charity are all one thing. Faith contains love and love contains faith.

CT: In contemplation there is faith and with this faith the journey is taking place from something known to unknown. It is happening naturally because of the movement of faith. In that journey scriptural revelation has an importance. And yet it seems to me that many people don't know the scripture.

Sr: I would modify that perhaps by saying that everyone has in one way or another the capacity to make the journey. The mediations may be different. You have different paths of different religions. I happen to be born into a Christian family. I can see perfectly well that this mediation can come through other religions. I think many people live their whole lives not even conscious of the faith they have. They don't even know it is there. Some have it in a different form. Mediation may not necessarily come through a religion as such. It can come through a multitude of things. I think that art may be a mediation that enables someone to touch a mystery without the person hardly knowing it. Sometimes I can see that faith grows and grows. It is one of those mysteries where we can't get very near.

CT: In Christian terminology one would say the primary mediator is Jesus. Where in this inwardness is the centrality of Jesus? Is it that Jesus inspired us to come to a contemplative faith or does the real work of Jesus begin during this period?

Sr: It can be either. I can imagine a person, without paying much attention to being a Christian, able to discover the reality of faith at some point and thereafter discover the reality of what the scripture contains. Other people who search inwardly without an object meet the gospels. Christ has said he will live in us. 'I will live in you. My father will live in you. My spirit is in you.' You might quite conceivably discover this before you have seen it in scripture. St John's Gospel is full of the word 'dwell'. 'Dwell in me and I will dwell in you.'

CT: Does that mean that one has to know about the historical person of Jesus?

Sr: As a Christian I believe in the historical Christ. But there are people who find God through a Christ they do not always see historically. In my perception of normal Christian living and understanding it's absolutely essential that one knows about the historical person of Jesus in order to find God.

CT: So one must know about his life, what he said and so on. His famous statement is, 'I am the way, the truth and the life and no one can reach the father except by me.' This has been a major hurdle for many people to understand.

Sr: God has all kinds of ways of telling us about himself. There are Christians who have very hazy notions about revelation, even false notions. If anyone says they are a Christian, it implies they are followers of Christ. It doesn't necessarily imply they know a lot of things. When you are born into a country which says it is Christian you take it for granted that all this has to be there in order to be Christian. Well, I don't feel like that because I think that God is much greater than all these things. I believe in Christ and I believe that God sent Christ. I know very little about historical proofs. I can know with a supernatural contact and very little human contact. Do you know what I mean?

CT: Are you speaking of a Christ which is discoverable by anybody even if he or she knows nothing of the scripture and has never seen the Bible?

Sr: The finding of Christ is the finding of God. If I find God I find

Christ. There I come to the truth. Christ's whole teaching was towards the father. He was leading people towards his father and he was leading them with the Spirit. How all of that is defined is another question. It is a question for theologians. A contemplative doesn't need all that detail. A contemplative contemplates God. Christ is there. You can ignore all of these specifics. I can be more precise about contemplation because I know the Gospels. I believe in an historical Christ. But I can well believe there are Buddhists and others who have a recognition of Christ in a very mysterious and quite undefinable way. Christ is more than just an historical person.

CT: When Christians find something too difficult to explain they often like to use the word 'mystery' as kind of catch-phrase or part of their religious rhetoric.

Sr: You know, life can go to a certain point and after that you cannot go any further, no matter how clever you are, no matter how marvellous your technique. You get to a point where you can't go any further. You can call it another name if you wish but it has to be called a mystery. It's very true that in Christianity we have tended to use incomprehensible words without explanation. Then people get on the defensive and put barriers where there aren't any really. Mystery comes into our life at all points. It comes into religion at certain levels that seem to be perfectly obvious. What would happen after death? You can make all sorts of explanations but if you haven't been there . . .

CT: When we go to deeper levels the sense of oneself, our ego structure, our personal history, all that we believe in seems to be increasingly less relevant. In that fading away and becoming nothing, self-negating in a natural way, would it be right to say only Christ can see God? All that is supposedly 'me' has no relationship to that state of contemplation which 'I' am unable to make or produce. In that there is Christ which begins to come into consciousness.

Sr: I'm not sure. I'll tell you why I'm not sure. Some of the early fathers declared absolutely that nobody could be a Christian unless they had experienced the Holy Spirit. And by experiencing the Holy Spirit they meant more than just believing the Holy Spirit. It's true that according to our scripture no one can see God and live.

CT: The scripture says, 'It is not I but Christ in me.'

Sr: If you go very deep the thought comes – what will be left when everything is gone, ourselves, this world and all the things that we have known? What would be left? We say 'God', and yet we can't see him. We can't touch him but I have Christ's word for it. What is the reality? I believe in the reality and yet, I can't see it. Only Christ can see it. And in that sense, when you say only Christ can see it, I believe it.

CT: You said you have Christ's word for it. Is that the scriptural word or does that mean something else to you?

Sr: It's not only the scriptural word but it's something which I have experienced as a Christian. Going back, I can see the point upon which I ultimately rely. I'm relying on the word that someone has said. Or else I am relying on an inward experience which I have had in which I can say, I know it. And I know this not because I read it. I know there is a presence in me. It has power because if I know it, it is impossible for it to be an illusion. A real experience of deep contemplation is something that you know and that is that.

CT: Does what one knows in deep contemplation always correspond to what is said in scripture?

Sr: Yes. That is why St Peter says that he is on the mountain with Christ at the transfiguration and he talks about it afterwards. He says that he saw the illumination of the Spirit and we have further confirmation of this through the words of the prophets. In other words, we have an experience which is personal yet confirmed from outside. I believe that is true of every kind of religious experience. If it were not we might be going around thinking that we are God.

CT: When a person has a deep, religious experience either through the contemplative process or in a particular moment, the mind easily takes hold of this. Then something can take place which creates narrow-mindedness.

Sr: That is the danger.

CT: I've seen quite a few people like this. Frankly I've told them, 'You were a more beautiful person before this experience. What happened to you?'

Sr: That I would say is proof that it wasn't really a completely genuine experience. It is difficult to discern true, spiritual experience. A true experience should have a certain criterion which can then be integrated into life. If you feel you've experienced the very Spirit, then show it to me. What are you doing with your life? That's a touchstone.

CT: You shall know them by . . .

Sr: . . . their fruits. When people begin to dogmatize I think it is a fairly certain sign that something is wrong. They may have had a true experience but they have not integrated it truly into their lives. Or they have let it deteriorate or added to it from outside. Some people have a peak experience and after that they try to live up to it. Some find they can't and finish up acting a role.

CT: So a person with a genuine religious experience can end up grasping hold of the experience to use it for self-affirmation. What makes the difference between a person who does integrate their experience and a person who doesn't?

Sr: A true experience should produce a true fruit. You live true to that light or you live in darkness. You have to go on living it in daily life. That's why people who have an experience of God, or who think they have, need some kind of support or check outside of themselves.

CT: What would be the support or check?

Sr: A spiritual friend.

CT: Which presumes that the spiritual friend . . .

Sr: . . . is already experienced. The spiritual friend must have trodden the road. The only genuine manifestation of a true experience of God is love. God *is* love. God is an overflowing of love. And our only way of living is by showing that love. That is why it is so terrible that so many religious people have an experience but are unable to love and give to others. They are not loving but selfish and dogmatic. Dogmatism is harmful and hurtful. You know as well as I do that we meet many people like that.

CT: Yes. In the inner transformation supported by faith I hear the statement of Jesus, 'No one can reach the father except by me.' 'Me' seems to mean love. Like finds like. Christ finds God. God finds Christ.

Sr: You can't see Christ without love and God is love. If you have faith as great as a mountain and you don't love, you are worth nothing. If you make all the noise in the teaching world, but you have no love, then it is nothing.

CT: So it seems that the inward journey must touch the places of love to understand transcendence. And then that love has to flow out into the world.

Sr: That's the only form of Christian contemplation that is possible. But it's not only Christian. It is Christian because it has the mediation of Christ. Buddhism has said that compassion is for all beings, but it does not always produce compassion. But that is another question.

The hope is that through contemplation you reach an attitude by which you serve others. Otherwise what are you doing?

CT: The bringing of love into the world seems to require a vehicle for that to happen.

Sr: Yes, that's true. It has to be channelled. If we all wanted to live life in any way I don't think we would accomplish much. It's true, we have to channel love in some form.

CT: Buddhism has kept, to a rather large degree, within the monastic system and so have the Christian contemplative orders.

Sr: The contemplative orders in Christianity tend to be too separate and communicate too little of their experience to others. I'm sure that at the beginning there was no such separation. It is simply an historical development. We need contemplation in the streets, centres of contemplation. It must flow out. There are sisters in Sydney, Australia who were originally a contemplative order. I asked them, 'How did you manage to get out of the enclosed convent and be allowed to work for others?' The superior there said, 'I was the Provincial and so I told them to go.' They went and what they're doing is marvellous. How can more of this communication come about?

CT: Buddhism has a long historical debate between the ideal of the *arahant* and the *bodhisattva*. The *arahant* is one who basically did nothing but contemplation so that the impurities of the mind were exhausted and freedom was found. There was no expectation on him or her to be active. Something of a spiritual protest took place during the centuries after the Buddha in which the *bodhisattva* ideal came to be. Men and women said it is not enough to meditate. Serving sentient beings became the thrust. This is one of the debates which is still not resolved.

Sr: I'm convinced that what is needed is contemplation and action. But many religious people would not be able to live as I'm living. Many need to live in a convent or with a community. When I first began to live alone in a flat like I'm living now, I was frightened because I had spent all those years in a convent. I had never fended for myself or earned my own living at all. Ten years ago I left the convent and had to learn how to cope with these things. I recognise the need for individual apostolates to do something alone and be connected with the community as well.

CT: My friend Francesca has been telling me about some of the hermits out in the countryside not so very far from Rome. I find it inspiring that there are people who are leading a solitary, contemplative life.

Sr: There are many hermits today. I've met some here and in England as well. I've always wished myself to be a hermit. I would go up into a mountain and that's that. However, I have a spiritual master and when I ask him if I can live in solitude he says no. He says go off sometimes for six months if you like but come back. So I live like this, with permission to live more free-style. I'm not living with as much structure as the other Christian nuns in the order. People come to me, I meet people, I write; I translate . . .

CT: Bringing the message of contemplation and action.

Sr: I am convinced now that this is what's needed.

CT: Thank you, Sister.

Beyond good and evil

An interview with Achaan Buddhadasa
Chai Ya, Thailand

A Poem

TO THE VOIDNESS

Do works of all kinds with a mind that is void
And then to the voidness give all the fruit
Take food of the voidness as do Holy Saints
And lo! You are dead to yourself from the very beginning.

In 1970 I went to visit Ven. Achaan Buddhadasa in his unfenced 250-acre forest monastery in Chai Ya, Surat Thani Province, twelve hours on the train south of Bangkok, Thailand. I asked him a question about meaning and purpose in life. I remembered he laughed and then said, 'If you really want to know then you have to first understand that there is nothing whatsoever worth grasping onto in life, nothing worth clinging to.' He then took hold of his monk's robe which was draped across his left shoulder, pulled it off and said, 'Not even this robe and the idea of being a monk is worth grasping.' He then called a novice over to take me to a hut deep in the forest and told me to reflect on what he had said.

Ven. Achaan Buddhadasa (Achaan means 'teacher' and Buddhadasa means 'servant of the Buddha') was ordained in 1926 when he was 20 and chose to live in a forest several miles from the present monastery. He engaged in both meditation and personal study of the talks of the Buddha, recorded in the Pali Canon which amounts to some twenty volumes. For the most part it was a very solitary life. He once told me that his only teacher and friend was the Buddha.

Nearly fifty years ago he moved to another forest which was only accessible by a dirt track and several miles from the nearest village. The people in the villages provided him a hut and each morning he would receive rice, coconut and vegetables from the homes of the farmers not far away.

As time went by, word got around about this solitary monk of Thai-Chinese origin living in the forest. Other monks came and requested permission from Ven. Buddhadasa to live near him in the forest. Nuns also came, so more huts were built. Lay people, first from the immediate area and then from all over the country, began to visit him. People began to record his talks which touched on every conceivable aspect of dharma, the teachings that deal with human existence. As the years went by, his discourses were transcribed into countless numbers of books. Some of them were translated into English, including *Handbook for Mankind, Heart-Wood from the Bo Tree, Towards the Truth, Mindfulness of Breathing* and *Why Were We Born?*

By the late 1980s, the number of visitors to Suanmoke Monastery had reached a staggering 300,000 per year, as coachloads of pilgrims visited the monastery, having travelled on the new trunk road just outside the forest. The number of huts for the monks had risen to more than a hundred, and a huge spiritual theatre hall and concrete ark had been built for the pilgrims to learn dharma on their visits. On a 50-acre nearby site a cloistered international meditation centre and a centre for inter-religious understanding is being built.

Meanwhile, Ven. Buddhadasa, Thailand's foremost religious speaker, poet and teacher continues to reside in the same spot as he did when he first arrived in the forest in the early 1940s. His hut has been replaced by a concrete building for him to receive guests. The Dalai Lama has paid him several visits.

In a traditional society like Thailand, Ven. Buddhadasa has always been regarded as both radical and controversial although a number of us who have lived with him in the forest regard his teachings as a valid inheritance of the Buddha's message. He has never permitted a temple to be built in the forest.

'If the ultimate truth returns the world will be bright; if it doesn't return the world is dark. But now the darkness has become ordinary.'

'The more incense and candles lit, the more it becomes superstition; at best, it's Buddhism for thumbsucking kids.'

'The more material progress the more insanity with the material; the more insane the more believing its progress.'

'The heart of Buddhism is on page one of the Bible.'

'Fools say that only time eats us and that we can't eat time.'

'Buddha can be anyone who awakens.'

When I arrived at Wat Suanmoke, it was 6.45 a.m. The dawn had just broken through. Outside the room of Achaan Buddhadasa were a party of some seventy college students seated on the ground. The

Achaan was seated cross-legged on a concrete bench talking to the students about education. He continues to sit there and talk as the people continue to come every day. He is 82 years old. A servant of the Buddha.

CT: What is the essence of dharma?

AB: When we speak of dharma, we speak of three things: natural phenomena, the law of nature and duty in accordance with the law of nature. Duty means taking the responsibility to solve the problems of life. It means engaging in right conduct to solve all problems of living.

CT: If a person is experiencing suffering or is faced with problems, what must he or she consider in order to engage in right conduct?

AB: Right conduct is to find out the case of the suffering. This is the duty of each person. This duty must be practised in accordance with the law of nature. Even the planet suffers the effect of impermanence, the effect that everything is changing all the time, and so everything has to be regarded as not self, only as nature. The concept of self is instinctive. Living beings have the instinct of self within.

CT: This instinct of self is so strong that it seems very difficult to see through.

AB: Instinct deceives humanity into believing that it has a real self. When instinct no longer deceives then the concept of self has no reality in the mind. A different kind of knowledge is then present in the mind. We can change from suffering to awakening. The instinct is neutral but it easily becomes defiled.

CT: Do we need to follow a gradual path of changing ourselves from being trapped in harmful and destructive instincts to enlightenment?

AB: It can happen suddenly.

CT: In spiritual teachings there is often an emphasis that desire and craving is the cause of suffering. In Western analysis, causes for human suffering are often regarded as political, social and economic. These are two different ways of understanding suffering.

AB: We have to know blind wanting. If the wanting is not blind but is simply to provide and sustain the basic requisites for life then it is not desire. This unenlightened ignorance creates desire and suffering. Desire for more and more gives birth to the concept of self – 'I' want, 'I' have. The 'I' is the blind wanting. Blindness wants. Ignorance wants. Ignorance wants more of itself. We have to be clear that it is this ignorance that wants all these things too, even nirvana.

CT: What do you think of social, political and economic wanting?

AB: Right wanting does not lead to selfishness.

CT: There are a growing number of people who are unhappy with property, power and possession, but they cannot see an alternative to that. They are also unhappy with religion.

AB: The question 'what is religion?' is an important one. I like to use an old definition of religion. Religion is observation and right conduct in order to blind a human being to the supreme thing. The supreme thing can be described as God or Nirvana. But now religion is full of ceremony and superstition; it is the religion of the fool, so it is not true religion. True religion is the same everywhere. In Christianity there is an important sentence at the beginning of the Bible. We must not eat from the tree of knowledge of good and evil. That means we must not attach to good and evil and discriminate in that way. There is this very high level of teaching in Christianity but today Christianity has forgotten that instruction.

CT: I first came to see you eighteen years ago and initially spent two or three weeks here. I said to you that I wanted to become a monk and you said, 'Anybody who changes their religion does so because they haven't understood their own.' Would you still say the same?

AB: The desire to change one's religion is ignorance at work. By means of wisdom, one will change oneself. Follow the steps of spiritual training of virtuous action, meditation and wisdom. This is called *sikkha* in the Pali language. It means look inside, see inside and know inside. It is to know yourself within, to know what is what. It is to know this 'I' and to know what is this problem of 'I', the problems of life. The true contentment is realizing that 'self' is truly 'not self'. 'Self' is 'not-self' already.

CT: This faith and wisdom you speak of seems to be of a different order. Often in religion, faith seems to be directed towards a God out there, or it is faith in the guru or a methodology. What you seem to be saying is that faith is present when we look within.

AB: Yes. Faith inside – look inside, see inside, know inside, know what is simply mental, emotional, physical activity and know it as just that. See into unwholesome activities of the mind. See into the suffering.

CT: Faith and *sikkha* contribute to wisdom?

AB: When we see and know what is what, then there is wisdom.

Wisdom is to know things directly and to know what to do and what not to do. What is especially important is to know this elusive 'self'. The 'self' is not to be regarded as a real 'self'. Only ignorance makes it seem to be a real 'self'. There is only body-mind and observation at work and any aspect of the human process can do its duty without 'self', without 'I'. There is no need to believe in 'self' or have a 'self'. Every aspect of mind-body is not 'self', not 'I'. But this is not nihilism.

CT: Does love and compassion come naturally when every aspect of life is seen to be void of 'self'?

AB: You have to know that even in love and compassion there can be 'self'. There is the 'self' who is the giver and there is the 'self' of the receiver. There may be love and compassion but this is not the supreme instruction, not the supreme thing. Love and compassion alone does not give emancipation or liberation. This was taught in India before the time of the Buddha. In love, there is a small scale 'self'.

CT: You have lived in this same spot for nearly fifty years. There was only the forest when you came. And today this enormous monastery without walls has built up around you while you have been sitting here. Why do you choose to give your life and your time to receiving countless numbers of people and teaching them dharma? What allows you to do this? You could have gone into the forest and never seen anybody. You could have lived as a recluse, but you have chosen to live and welcome all these people.

AB: By means of wisdom. Not by means of attachment to 'self'. It is to know what to do and what not to do.

CT: But couldn't some other monk say, 'By means of wisdom I choose to live in solitude.' Your life has been very available for people to come to see you.

AB: It's convenience only. [*Laughing.*] Some friends or some people come for some instruction.

CT: Isn't that love and compassion?

AB: One does not have to attach oneself to love and compassion. There is simply duty through wisdom.

CT: One of the criticisms of Buddhism is that we can spend so much time engaged in looking within that we forget about nuclear bombs, we forget about the destruction of the rainforests and poverty and pain elsewhere.

AB: If we do not see the reality of the mind-body then we cannot stop false and harmful views, harmful thinking and ignorance. We then cannot know the right way of living. We become too much attached to good and evil. Don't use the word 'detached'. To be detached is another kind of attachment. It is to be detached from one thing by means of another attachment. This only makes a new problem.

CT: Yes. I can understand that.

At the present time there is a lot of discussion between people of different religions. What does Buddhism have to learn from Christianity and do you think that Christianity can learn from Buddhism?

AB: Both can learn from each other to discover mutual understanding. I learnt the utmost important principle from one single sentence in the Book of Genesis: God commanded the couple not to eat of the tree of good and evil. That sentence is the essence and heart of Buddhism. That means not to be enslaved by the value given to good and evil. It is to go beyond the influence of good and evil, beyond positivism and negativism and thus be free and emancipated. That is the heart of Buddhism. Christians did not understand this. They became attached to the instruction of Jesus Christ to love one another. Owing to attachment to good and evil, selfishness occurs. We give up selfishness by not being attached to good and evil. Then in the end of this attachment, we love others automatically.

CT: Some people might say, for example, that the work to save the rainforest, the work to save animals from the laboratories, the work to help people's struggle for peace and justice is doing good as opposed to evil.

AB: If they are attached to doing good they have not realised that ultimately there really is not good nor evil, only suchness. Out of wisdom comes action where events are not interpreted as good and bad. First, be beyond good and bad.

CT: Let me give one example where wisdom and action is required. At the present time in Thailand there is the possibility of a huge dam being built. The authorities say the dam will provide electricity to many people, but the protestors say that the dam will destroy thousands of acres of forest. This seems to be an issue of right conduct. What is your response? Do we have a dam or do we protect the rainforest?

AB: Not correct. This is surplus knowledge.

CT: Surplus knowledge?

AB: Material progress will destroy everything. They think they are doing good but it is selfishness of human beings. Selfishness destroys sentient beings, through the support of ignorance. The problem is inside, so that is where we have to look. The selfishness, the suffering, the cause of suffering and the cessation of it is within.

CT: What do you see in contemporary society as the role of the monk or nun?

AB: Their role is to be an example of living a life beyond all problems so that others will look within and live in the same way. Selfishness in the world is to be destroyed, otherwise the world will be destroyed. Now selfishness rules the world.

CT: How do you feel about the destruction that is happening on the earth?

AB: No need to be unhappy or happy. We do our duty by means of wisdom and abide in suchness, not in good and evil, not in positive and negative thinking. To help our friends in the whole world to know the dharma is to direct them beyond the influence in the world of positive and negative. So that our friends have a free life, an emancipated life, a liberated life. May all our friends in the world know this.

CT: These days I travel extensively giving dharma teachings. I feel grateful to you for your teachings. For many years you have emphasised seeing through 'I', 'me' and 'mine' and the discovery of suchness.

AB: To be beyond the influence of positive and negative we have to be void of 'self'. We must know the concept of 'self'. To see 'self' is to know that it is not a real thing but a concept. We come from the mother's womb. After that the senses make contact with this or that and then the wanting takes place in the mind which is positive or negative. This takes place more and more and more. Then the 'I' arises; this delusive appearance is believed to be more than a concept. The emancipated mind is emancipated from this delusion of the reality of 'self'. 'I' is not a real thing; the 'I' is only language. Even the Buddha uses the concept 'I' or 'he' or 'she' but without attachment to giving any meaning to the term. The concept is used just to speak with people in the street because that is the language used. It is to make sense of speaking and thinking.

CT: What is the difference between the two? The 'I' arises when speaking and the 'I' arises when thinking.

AB: Language is for the person who has 'self' and language is for the person who knows 'not-self'. Spiritual teachings need to be in harmony with natural truth. I prefer to see Buddhism, Christianity and other religions as a natural truth to serve sentient beings, to solve the problems of suffering through not being under the control of positivism and negativism.

CT: Can I make a small suggestion? Could the title of your book *Handbook for Mankind* be changed to *Handbook for Humankind?* In the West now, we do not use the word 'mankind' much at all. We are all human beings.

AB: Is human being better than sentient being? [*Laughing.*]

CT: We have forgotten we are human beings and we have become human havings and human wantings.

AB: Then we are not yet human beings, not yet human. We have the wrong system of education in this nation and in the whole world. Education only teaches young people to be clever. They learn knowledge in order to command cleverness, cleverness in selfishness. The teachers cannot govern their own cleverness. The world will be destroyed by cleverness. Teach them to know selfishness, the demon, the satan of human life. It is peculiar that the human world has much more selfishness than the animal world. It is rather funny. We say we are civilised; we are always saying we are more civilised than animals but we have much more selfishness. Teach there is 'not-self' so that there is 'not-selfishness'.

CT: Thank you, Achaan.

Language and silence

An interview with Maurice Ash
Totnes, Devon, England

Maurice Ash, founder of the Sharpham Trust and author of *Journey through the Eye of the Needle*, lives at Sharpham House, Ashprington, three miles south of Totnes. During the 1980s Totnes was labelled by the media as Britain's 'New Age capital'. In 1990, BBC2 television made a documentary on the social experiment taking place in the area.

In a book published in the late 1980s, *Spilling the Beans*, Martin Stott writes: 'The area of Britain to live is in Devon. There are more natural healers, holistic health practitioners, alternative therapists and other inner-directed souls to the square mile [there] than any other part of the country. South Devon is better than North Devon. The Totnes-Ashburton area is the veritable Californian Marin county of Britain. Living there is what all AT's [alternative types] ultimately aspire to.'

Maurice Ash would certainly be considered one of the people who established alternative values in the area. In the early 1960s Maurice, his wife Ruth and their three daughters moved to Sharpham House, a large English country house situated on six hundred acres of beautiful countryside facing the River Dart and close to the village of Ashprington.

Ruth Ash came on her mother's side from the Whitney family, a well-known family in the United States. She was formerly Ruth Elmhirst, whose parents founded the Dartington Hall Trust in the mid 1920s – a many-sided progressive experiment in rural life, inspired by Rabindranath Tagore. Dartington attracted artists of the calibre of the American Mark Tobey, Bernard Leach and The Ballet Joos. Well-known people such as Bertrand Russell, Barbara Hepworth, Aldous Huxley and Sean O'Casey sent their children to the school.

In 1964 Maurice became a trustee of Dartington Hall Trust and was chairperson from 1972-1984. He has also been chairperson of the Town and Country Planning Association, was founder chairperson of the Green Alliance, and is a member of the Henry Moore Foundation.

Maurice was born in Bihar, India, in 1917, where his father served the Raj. He later went on to study economics at the London School of Economics. During World War II, Maurice served the British Army in the Egyptian desert and in Italy and Greece. In the tanks he was involved in action, but he says it was not so much the battle as the waiting for it that is his most lasting impression of that period.

Along with members of his family, Maurice has been a pillar of support for many valuable projects in the Totnes area. One of the central tenets of Green thought is, 'act locally, think globally', and Maurice has applied this tenet to a remarkable degree. He is the author of *New Renaissance, Green Politics, A Guide to the Structure of London* and *Who Are The Progressives Now?*

Maurice is chairperson of the Sharpham Trust – a trust established to facilitate the use of the Sharpham Estate in an alternative and skilful way. Projects include organic farms and a spiritual community that occupies the top floor of his home. At the present time, the Trust is expanding its meetings, workshops and seminars on issues relevant to our time. In 1970s the Findhorn Community played an important role in the communication of alternative values. The Sharpham Estate, alongside the Dartington Trust and Totnes, may well play a similar role for the 1990s.

This interview focuses on three areas. One is the influence of Ludwig Wittgenstein (the Austrian philosopher) and Buddhism on Maurice's way of perceiving the world. In *Who's Who* he lists as his recreation, 'applying Wittgenstein', which, he would admit, is something Wittgenstein himself might not have deemed possible. The second area of focus is on the problems, either in the present or future, facing the Dartington Trust; and the third is on his willingness to begin a whole new project right on his doorstep – the Sharpham Estate.

Even though the interview focuses largely on the local situation here in Devon, it seems to me that there are important factors to be learnt with regard to thought, language, communication and the application of these ideas. Hopefully the interview will stimulate reflections on the process of life rather than on the apparent separateness of issues, people and things.

The interview with Maurice was conducted at his home a few weeks after his 70th birthday. He has converted one small corner of the mansion into what is now virtually a one-bedroom flat for his personal use.

CT: I would like to ask you about some of your formative influences. Could we begin with Ludwig Wittgenstein? Why did Wittgenstein have such an influence on you?

MA: The formative influences don't start with Wittgenstein, of course. He only had the effect of destroying some of the previous influences in my life. My discovery of Wittgenstein and the learning from his writings date back about thirty years to 1957 or 1958. He demonstrated the impossibility of the search that I had been engaged in for the previous twenty years, since my university days or even before. It was a search to put together some kind of comprehensive social science. I studied pure economics and I thought the methods of economics could be applied to the social sciences generally. So I was engaged in a theory of history, somewhat influenced originally by Tolstoy's writings. In Tolstoy's *War and Peace*, there are fifty pages at the end which are devoted to his theory of history, if I remember rightly. I would say, though, that the influence of Tolstoy, in other ways, has remained much more important. In the wake of World War II, anyway, I was primarily concentrating upon a theory of international relations, a theory of the balance of power.

CT: Was this theory simply the development of a personal world view or was it that you were actively engaged in the balance of power and international relations?

MA: I was entirely detached. That was the whole point of the impact of Wittgenstein. He demonstrated this fact to me. He made me seriously suspect that neither economics nor any social science can be conducted from the position of the detached observer. While I was working on this thesis in 1957 I was involved in running a small farm in Essex with my wife Ruth. We had a farm because I thought it was simply not enough to be engaged in this private research. We ought to be involved in the everyday world, so to speak. We were living in the countryside north of London and sought to become involved in the life there.

I should say here that it wasn't Wittgenstein himself that influenced me but a book, *The Idea of a Social Science* by Peter Winch, based on the writings of Wittgenstein. It is by no means unusual that one approaches Wittgenstein indirectly, through another.

CT: I have Wittgenstein's *Philosophical Investigations* and I find it very difficult to read.

MA: If it's any consolation I am reviewing at the present two books on Wittgenstein. One is part-authored by a former student of his in the late 1940s, Stephen Toulmin. He says that anybody who didn't actually attend Wittgenstein's lectures must be forgiven for not understanding what he is writing about. That is a measure of how radical it is. So I set myself the task of understanding what he was writing about. I began with the *Tractatus* which I find, like you, virtually unintelligible. Then I tried to read *Philosophical Investigations*, and then I continued to read various commentators. Meanwhile I was occupied with the practicalities of our farm. I suppose as a result of Wittgenstein's influence I virtually abandoned all previous models, based on the mechanistic view, to compose a new theory of the balance of power between nation states. I had actually written a book. It's somewhere in the attic I suppose, if the mice haven't enjoyed it . . .

CT: What happened next?

MA: By the process of abandoning the old models, my attention was drawn to Zen writings in the 1960s. I don't know how that first happened.

CT: What comes to mind when you think of Wittgenstein and his analysis of thought and language as compared with the perception and aesthetics of Zen? Is there a commonality between the two?

MA: Yes, enormously so. The book by Chris Gudmunsen, *Wittgenstein and Buddhism*, sets it out. If you read the last five pages of the *Tractatus*, after having gone through the logic of language and all that brain-cracking stuff, you come to a lot of Zen. For example, Wittgenstein says (I have the book here): 'All propositions are of equal value.' By that he means that propositions are statements about fact. They relate to that which language can explain which is within the world. All that he called of value, however, lies outside the world. Wittgenstein was concerned to show the limits of language, so to speak. His followers almost unanimously thought that only what is within the limits of language is important. What *he* thought was that all that actually mattered was *outside* the limits of language.

CT: So a common factor is that Zen meditation resolutely sees through the field of thought and language.

MA: It is not just Zen but the whole Buddhist tradition, especially the Mahayana and the teachings of Nagarjuna [the second-century saint-philosopher]. Wittgenstein and Nagarjuna are not saying things the same way and yet they come to the same point – of silence. Nearly 2000 years earlier than Wittgenstein, Nagarjuna had arrived at this point. Wittgenstein knew nothing about 'meditation' and arrived at it from an entirely different route.

In Wittgenstein's case it was through logic and the limits of logic. When you come to the limits of logic you come to silence and to truth as it is lived. He writes, 'The sense of the world must lie outside the world and in the world everything is as it is and everything happens as it does happen. In it no value exists – and if it did exist it would have no value. If there is any value that does have value it must lie outside the whole sphere of what happens and is the case. For all that happens and is the case is accidental.' You can probably get a sense of Zen coming through.

CT: Yes. Is there another quotation?

MA: 'My propositions serve as illustrations in the following way: anyone who understands me eventually recognizes them as nonsensical when he has used them as steps to climb up beyond them. He must, so to speak, throw away the ladder as he has climbed up it. He must transcend these propositions and then he will see the world aright.' Well, isn't that extremely like Zen? In Zen it is said, 'Before I knew Zen there were rivers and mountains. While I practised Zen, rivers were no longer rivers and mountains were no longer mountains. After Zen, rivers were rivers and mountains were mountains.' What we cannot speak about we must pass over in silence. It's mystical writing of the most powerful sort.

CT: Then after these influences you moved to South Devon and to Dartington Hall.

MA: Ruth wanted to come back home to Dartington. We spent two years setting up the estate at Sharpham. In 1964 I was asked to become a trustee of Dartington and three years later I also became chairman of the Town and Country Planning Association. I felt that rural and urban planning should be holistic. It's a different way of looking at the world from the reductionist norm in planning. Theoretically, I think you should look at the totality of a town, city or village as a whole so the norms of reductionist measurement don't apply. You're concerned with the form, and hence the quality.

CT: Do you mean the aesthetics of the form?

MA: It's not actually visual aesthetics that one is concerned with. You can call it 'aesthetics', stretching the term considerably. It has more to do with social rather than physical form. It has to do with social justice and harmony.

CT: What did you actually perceive taking place in town and country planning that was affecting the quality of people's lives?

MA: I suppose in today's language it was 'community,' although in those days that was almost a dirty word. I was concerned with the loss of community and the rediscovery of community, including the loss of community in the great cities as well as concern about the squalor of them. There was also the attempt to rediscover communities through new towns and new villages. I was supportive of new towns and villages but I wasn't supportive of the way the legislation was drawn up or implemented.

CT: Let us turn to the local situation. You have said that Dartington School got stuck and lost its way. What happened?

MA: The organisations and institutions that grew at Dartington began to take over. The College, for example, became concerned with the business of survival as a college. The various facets of Dartington, whether the businesses, the education or the arts were all fixed in their separate moulds. The original vision was to ensure an inter-connectedness throughout the estate and all the activities on it. But that inter-connectedness had long since gone and was becoming more and more difficult to recapture. It was all spinning apart, as happens with specialisms.

CT: Don't institutions become bureaucratic and concerned with the quest for survival? What can safeguard against that?

MA: These things certainly happen in our culture of reductionism and specialization. The only thing that held Dartington together was the personality of its founders. I'll give you an illustration. Around 1970, after Leonard Elmhirst had gone to America and I had become chairman, Royston Lambert became head of Dartington School. He invited a lot of people along to his house for a social evening. Among the people invited was Peter Cox, who had been at Dartington since before the war. At one point in that evening he turned to me with an amused expression and said, 'This is the first time I have ever been inside this house or that the head of the College has even been into the School.' That is an indication of the way it had actually gone . . . to smithereens.

CT: What I hear is a criticism of the detached and isolated observer position. In specialization there tends to be a loss of connectedness so that one isn't deeply familiar with everything else that is happening around.

MA: Yes, that is true. Because Leonard and Dorothy were still there when I first came on the scene, people dimly and vaguely held to the notion of the wholeness of the estate. People talked, and perhaps still talk, about 'the estate' in a rather mystical way – and that is something very precious.

CT: Are you saying that the visionary is needed to sustain something which people who come later don't have?

MA: I don't think so. If I thought that I would despair. I think the initial energy and impulse had long since drained out of Leonard and Dorothy themselves. It was, simply, that other people saw them as the symbol of the whole for which they yearned. A connectedness can be sustained if people understand each other's language. This reverts to a Wittgensteinian view. We need to understand the limits of the languages we use to pursue the various specializations that divide us; given this understanding people would empathise with one another. And this empathy was absent at Dartington. The wholeness was there but not actively so. Yet it did make of the estate an absolute, a form of life.

CT: Are you saying that the field of language and the way we communicate with each other is the essential factor towards wholeness?

MA: I think so, just in as far as the fallacy of our culture is that words describe reality. As people pursue their specialisms they each have their own language for their own specialism. Then people become so oblivious to the truth that they don't have a monopoly of the meanings of the words they use.

CT: What would be an example of this?

MA: A most obvious example is the word 'wealth'. People involved in the creation of 'wealth' through economic, business and commercial activities are really oblivious to the fact that 'wealth' can have a very different meaning for other people. 'Land' can have a very different meaning for people who are not farmers than it has for farmers. 'Education' has a very different sense for people who are not professional teachers. 'Art' has become a divisive thing. Instead of the arts being the cement that joined the Dartington Community, as the Elmhirsts had hoped, they were the main cause of driving the community apart. People down in the village rejected the notion of art that was being practised up at Dartington Hall.

My concern at Dartington was not to say the purpose of Dartington is XYZ. There is no single purpose you can find for a diverse and complex community like that, at least in my judgment. I wanted people to come to an awareness that what they *thought* they were doing was ultimately not materially real, that the language they were using did not actually picture reality, so to speak. All that we do is actually imbued with mystery. We are all equally ignorant of what 'reality' is. Mine was a concern which I don't think anybody understood. It was a concern that we should share our ignorance. It is in that concern, I feel, that some kind of spiritual life could be generated – out of our ignorance, not out of our knowledge and its pride.

CT: Something can emerge out of enlightened ignorance where one has no fixed view nor purpose.

MA: I think so, but for this to happen I think we have to live in communities that are not too large or too complex. If the places people live, like in the great cities, continue to be as they are, then there will never be silence. A few people living together might come to an understanding that their different activities are somehow not real; therefore what they really have in common is a silence. I'm not explaining this well, but because of the chatter of a complex city, one will never discover that 'silence' there.

CT: If all activities are somehow unreal then surely it wouldn't enliven the heart to an expanded vision and awareness. Is it perhaps more accurate to say, activities are not *ultimately* real? Our activities are not as significant as the way we *think* they are?

MA: Well, it certainly brings into question the very concept of 'reality'. The concept of 'reality' has been our ruling concept for the last 2000 years in the West. Western philosophy has been posited on the notion of atomistic things, rather than of process, as real. But perhaps all we can do is play games with the word.

CT: In that respect to go from describing and thinking about 'things' to an understanding of process would be a significant shift. What we are emphasising is the way we think and talk.

MA: Yes.

CT: In the last five years you have turned your focus of attention more towards the Sharpham Estate.

MA: I left Dartington for the nominal reason that I was of an age at which I could no longer be responsible for so many people and activities. I think that's fairly sound in principle anyway. On a deeper level I left because of a sadness at the spiritual vacuum at the heart of Dartington. There was no silence, there was no consciousness of our ignorance, or that we partook of a mystery in this world. Since I remained concerned with rural life I have all the way through held on to neo-Tolstoian values. I have been concerned with the meaning of our relationship to the natural world. I think that concern is here at Sharpham as it was in Dartington in the early days.

CT: Gandhi was of course substantially influenced by Tolstoy. When I think of Tolstoy's values I think of self-reliance, self-sufficiency, creativity and voluntary simplicity. Is that what you are referring to?

MA: Yes, absolutely. A rather amusing aside to this is that I think Rabindranath Tagore was also influenced by Tolstoy. Tagore and Elmhirst were very close and worked together. Wittgenstein came back into philosophy when he was enticed in the late twenties by the Vienna Circle of philosophers. They thought Wittgenstein was the apostle of positivism: that is, a scientific and empirical view of reality. In that respect they completely misunderstood what he was driving at. Nevertheless when he met the circle he both mystified and offended them. In his first meeting with them he did not discuss philosophy but read the poems of Tagore. They were completely nonplussed by this.

CT: So, the traces of influences are through Tolstoy, Wittgenstein and Buddhism. Are you integrating spirit and matter into your vision of Sharpham?

MA: I don't know that I have a vision, quite honestly. I have a concern. To some extent I suppose you could look at it in terms of what Schumacher called his 'lifeboat theory'. In a collapsing world a few lifeboats should be launched from the sinking Titanic. Actually, I don't go along with that theory. I think it is a policy of despair. I am much more optimistic than that. I am, of course, pessimistic for the future of our urban, industrialized, reductionistic, materialistic society. Nevertheless, human common sense and feeling will prevail. But it will be very painful.

CT: What is despairing about the situation? Why do you say change will be painful?

MA: We had a foretaste of the pain a few weeks ago with the crash on the Stock Exchange. That's only the beginning. The question now is: Will such a crash lead to a depression? It does indicate a possible path of disintegration, especially taken in conjunction with the drug problem. Our society is entirely ephemeral. Here at Sharpham I hope to create something of a model, if you like, for how life might be reordered within a disintegrating society. We have, for instance, five agricultural holdings on the estate: contrary to the conventional wisdom, we have not made our units larger, we have made them smaller. We hope that each unit will struggle for survival better on its own, rather than if it was under management. Furthermore we wanted to bring more people back to the land, so we have more activities, like cheese-making, adding value.

CT: Basically you have a number of partnerships and that is a common thread within the estate.

MA: That is just the structural device. The estate is being entrusted – some of it is already entrusted to the Sharpham Trust – so that when I am gone there will be a continuity of ownership and policy, all within the same framework.

CT: On the Sharpham Estate, you have some people who, I'm sure, are spiritually much more akin to you than others. The Buddhist community upstairs would be an example. Then there are others whose kinship with you is through the land. How do you relate to these differences?

MA: This is the spirit/matter thing. I don't recognize a significant distinction between the two. I don't think they can live just a material life or just a spiritual life. They are both meaningless when thought of as separate from each other. The people who have been attracted to work on the land here may not be Buddhists but they have a spiritual component to the work they do. Most are, for instance, imbued with the ideas of organic farming; one is using Rudolf Steiner's bio-dynamic approach to the land. There is certainly a non-materialistic component to their work. The people on the land may not use the same words as the community upstairs, but they share a spiritual core to their lives.

CT: So at Sharpham you have overt spirituality – the community meditates, explores spiritual thought, puts on workshops and seminars. You also have an intrinsic spirituality in the attitudes of the people on the estate in terms of the activities in which they are engaged. Now the Trust and others here are having meetings with regard to the arts. Is it your intention to explore and open up the possibilities of bringing the arts to Sharpham?

MA: When you start from zero there is such a long way to go. I think the question of the aesthetic in life is significant. The question of the arts is not of the arts as we know them today, which are irredeemably corrupt. The aesthetic of life is implicit in the whole project here. The poetic seems to me to be the medium of reconciliation between language and the world. We have gone so far in our culture from the poetic. I'm not at all sure that the rot didn't set in when we learnt to write. [*Laughing.*] Take the Celtic legends, for instance. It was a matter of principle for the Celts that their legends were not transcribed. In Islam likewise they say that to take a photograph of somebody is to take away their spirit. To write down legends for the Celts was to take away their souls.

CT: You say this but you are a great lover of literature, you write and review books and you use language to a considerable degree.

MA: One is a prisoner of one's world; I recognise that. The same criticism was levelled against Wittgenstein. (Please don't read any comparison into that!) He went out of his way to discourage his students from doing philosophy. The same question was put to him: Why don't you stop doing philosophy? He did say in *Philosophical Investigations* that the point of philosophy is to know when to stop doing it. His answer was that he was not hurting anyone else but himself by being a philosopher. This is not an adequate answer. I'm just speculating that when writing was discovered, the poetic began to be lost to the world. Literacy creates an arid silence between people. In literacy there is too easily a lack of relationship.

CT: We do seem to be losing the tradition of expressing the poetic. In some of the Eastern traditions the smallest gesture is worthy of total mindfulness. Washing dishes is as worthy of participation as *any* other activity and responsibility. Is the poetic being discovered at Sharpham?

MA: Gosh, I would like to think it might be. The discussions about the arts are tending towards that. The discussions are not about, say, adult education classes in drawing or pottery. They have to do with mindfulness in everyday life. We should however be careful of, say, studying the tea ceremony, because it puts the making of a cup of tea into a separate compartment, separate from everyday life.

CT: It is another example of specialization. Your interpretation of the meaning of the arts is not as a stereotyped specialization, but as the language of expressing something beautiful in the ordinary.

MA: Yes, absolutely. One other thing I should say about leaving Dartington and starting these activities at Sharpham: Ruth and I had this place and I have always felt this really — that there is no justification for a house of this kind for just one family. A house like this must be a focus and a centre of service. We try to interpret what that means in this day and age and what kind of service a place like this can provide.

For the last three hundred years, the English country house has represented appropriation for private glory, wealth and, above all, power by landowners. Houses like this have been self-indulgent – contrary to the myths. There has been a great betrayal by the gentry.

CT: It seems to me an unusual expression of trust to open the doors and make the entire top floor of one's home available to a group of people that you don't know, especially when living in the rooms below. Where does that spirit, that trust come from?

MA: I think that is perfectly normal to humankind. It is only in a suspicious and untrusting culture, as in cities, where one gets mugged and robbed. In rural areas people are more trusting of one another. My mind goes back to the monasteries. The monastery is much more the model for us than even the best of English country houses. Having said that, I don't want to denigrate everything that has happened in our culture for the last few hundred years, nor ever to the old monastic pattern.

CT: You are working to make the best use of the various resources which you have.

MA: I want to help reinspirit the countryside in another way than by the old relationship of clergy to manor house. As far as agriculture is concerned the crisis is already with us. I want to show there's a spiritual core to rural life.

CT: Thank you, Maurice.

SOCIAL AWARENESS

A free and protected space

An interview with Dora Kalff
Zurich, Switzerland

I rather appreciated a description I read of Dora Kalff that said, 'Mrs Kalff is a friend of the unconscious.' Mrs Kalff's work with sandplay therapy for children and adults gained international recognition among Jungian therapists and clients alike. And this recognition came through her remarkable capacity to relate to clients at a deep level both in a personal way and symbolically.

If we make a division between the conscious mind and unconscious, and some of us regard it as a conceptual division, we may describe the unconscious as a field rich in imagery, memory and symbolism. The skill of Mrs Kalff was to provide a free and protected space so that the child or adult could permit the deep emotions, projections and fantasies to surface into the conscious world knowing that they would be accepted without judgement or rejection.

Mrs Kalff was born in 1903 and died in January 1990. She spent five years from 1943 to 1948 living in the Swiss Alps with her two children, Martin and Peter, and this is where she first came into contact with the family of Carl Jung. In the late 1950s, after finishing her training as a Jungian analyst and moving to England to continue her studies, she was introduced to sandplay therapy by the creator of this tool, Dr Margaret Lowenfeld.

For more than thirty years hundreds of clients of all ages and background went to the home of Mrs Kalff for therapy. The countless little figures made up of people from around the world – animals, trees, vehicles, religious symbols, toys and other items – were housed by the thousands on the shelves in her room. The sand trays and figures were the tools which provided the opportunity for the imagination to flow.

To participate in a session of sandplay therapy, as I did, was to participate in what seems to be a timeless ritual of exploration. One simply did not know what one's inner responses would be to the countless figures on display when Mrs Kalff invited one to choose. During a session during which Mrs Kalff said little there was a pervasive atmosphere of silence, stillness and an attentive warmth.

In her book, *Sandplay*, Mrs Kalff outlined ten cases, mostly with children, which attempted to illustrate the experience, actual as well as symbolic, that occurred within her free and protected space. The 75 photographs showing the figures placed in the sandtray reveal the diversity of unexpressed feelings and imagery within that most of us can relate to. One photograph showed a sandtray full of (toy) weapons. Another showed isolated homes along with different forms of transport in a traffic jam. Another showed a farm with two black ravens. Mrs Kalff observed through the years that by providing an atmosphere for individuals to be totally themselves while engaging in play, fresh and creative energies begin to flow through the heart and mind and contribute substantially to being an integrated human being.

Mrs Kalff's method with the sandtray has two parts to it. One is to make the setting in the tray and the second is for the client to tell the story if he or she so wishes. I found in my experience with the therapy that the whole process is so meditative that, like making a good meal, one wishes to share it with another. So after moving a handful of figures to the sandtray – it must have taken twenty minutes in the silence for me to pick out a small number of figures – I felt a strong wish to talk with Mrs Kalff about what the figures and the final scene in the tray meant for me.

Very kindly, she revealed some of her perceptions to me of what she saw in the sandtray. It is not something she would normally do. As she pointed out, it is necessary to see the unconscious through a number of sandtrays and not to isolate one interpretation. The tray itself is not large by any means. Sitting in front of the tray enables one to view the tray, the sand and contents without having to move the eyes from side to side. This contributes to a focused, meditative attention which enables the deeper inner life to flow out through the hands and into the tray.

As Jung and others have recognised, the imagination is a remarkable key to self-knowledge. In a way, the figures in the sandtray are all interacting with the imaginative processes and this provides the link to self-understanding. To put it in another way, what you see is what you are, in that moment of facing the sandtray.

The meeting with Mrs Kalff and the sandplay session that I participated in still retains a freshness to it as I write two and a half years later. In the first part of the interview, Mrs Kalff speaks about her work and the background to it and the second part of the interview is the transcription of my session with her.

CT: When did you become a Jungian therapist?

DK: I began my studies after World War II. I had experienced such hardship during the war, and afterwards Switzerland was so normal that I felt I couldn't deal with this normality. I had to go away somewhere to recover so I retired to the mountains with my two children because I love the mountains. My husband was still in Holland at that time. He died shortly after the war and so I stayed with a nurse because I did not have any knowledge about how to deal with children. The only person I could really talk to was the young pastor of the village. We had lengthy discussions on philosophy.

CT: At this time, had you made contact with Carl Jung?

DK: No, not yet. It so happened that the place that I had chosen to stay was the holiday place of Jung. So, eventually I got to know the family. Mrs Belman, who is the daughter of Jung, is very good with horoscopes. She did my horoscope and she decided that I should study Jungian psychology. I had to earn money. So I said, 'OK, I shall study this psychology,' but I did not want to leave this nice place in the mountains. It was a simple hut. I had never lived like that before. I had all the freedom. I went for long walks with or without the children. I decided to go for half the week down to Zurich and study at the Institute and half the week I would stay up in the mountains. But it was too difficult for my health to go up and down the mountains in such a short time. So we had to decide to find a house in Zurich. It was not easy. They all said, you have two children, and I would get very discouraged. Then Francian, the son of Jung who was an architect, offered to build a house for me. He asked me what I would want and I said, 'I want a house with windows like the old farmhouses in Switzerland. I would like to have a madonna and I would like to have a vine growing outside.' He laughed and said it was very easy to build a house like that. But I said, actually, I prefer to have an old house. When I began looking, a house was offered to me and it had a row of windows, a madonna outside and a vine grows there. I knew it was the right house!

CT: Did you start working with Jung?

DK: I only worked partly with Jung. I spent a lot of time with Mrs Jung. She was my analyst. I completed the training in about 1956 and then went to England to study more about child psychology and this is where I discovered sandplay therapy. I met Dr Margaret Lowenfeld, a psychiatrist who ran a child guidance clinic in London, who is the creator of the tool of sandplay therapy. She was using it mainly as a diagnostic tool and was not using it with Jungian archetypes.

CT: So you took sandplay therapy from the classic psychiatry tradition into a Jungian interpretation?

DK: In a way, one might say, yes. Dr Lowenfeld was not a Jungian. I was excited to set up my own practice to use this tool combining it with Jung's ideas so I went back to Zurich and began receiving clients.

CT: How many figures or models did you begin with?

DK: Maybe this shelf here. [*Hundreds.*] At the beginning I was working with children. Children were always being sent to me because of difficulties at school. Parents and teachers think that children have to learn something about schooling. I found that there are much deeper disturbances behind their difficulties. I discovered very quickly that when you watch children *play* you know more about them. When they play regularly in the sand they undergo a process which seems to go into the depth of the unconscious.

CT: When parents see their children experiencing difficulties at school, what is this in regard to their studies, their relationship with the teacher, their relationship with other children?

DK: The main complaint is usually lack of concentration. They cannot study well and they cannot follow the lessons, which concerns the parents and teachers. Some are sent to me by doctors. I work with children from 4 to 18 years old. It is very often the case that the younger child does not want the parent to leave. So in the first hour the parent can always come and sit in. Maybe after an hour and a half the child says, 'You can leave, mummy.' Sometimes the child wants to have mummy here two or three hours. I just leave it free.

CT: How do you personally make contact with the children? Is it immediately through the models and figures?

DK: No. I create what I call a free and protected space for the one that comes in here, child or adult. They have to feel completely free and accepted. You have to put aside all criticism, all judgment and just fully accept whoever comes to you in here. It's like compassion in Buddhism, isn't it? They must feel free. I talk to them and tell them that here are a lot of figures and here is a sand box. Some think they are too old to play in the sandtray. They say, that is OK for my little brother but not for me.

CT: How do you get them to respond?

DK: I might say, 'You know, sometimes you have a nice idea and you don't know where it comes from and other times you know. Here you have sand. You can move the sand about and then if you like you can take the figures and play with them in the sand.' And then these ideas come and get activated.

CT: With a child there would probably be more spontaneity than with an adult. I noticed with myself when I walked into the room and looked at the figures, the first thought was, 'What figures would I choose?' So it is not quite from play but more from an initial thought.

DK: I work with some initial structure. I would never say, 'Do anything in the sand.' First, I show you the two trays filled with sand and then I say, 'In this tray the sand is a little damp and in this tray the sand is completely dry. Put your hand in and feel what is agreeable.' You begin with this. You begin to see what is happening with the sand as it is moved. The bottom of the tray is painted blue so sometimes when you get to the bottom you get the idea of water. Then maybe you get the idea of a hill or you get the idea of movement in landscape. You think, 'What is this?' I don't say anything. Then maybe you feel there should be a house or a tree or human being or an animal. Then you get the figure you want.

What happens in the sand is a kind of image or picture which is sometimes called sand pictures or sand painting. Then I need to understand the symbolic language in all of the things that they put in the sand and the forms they make in the sand.

CT: How do you transfer this understanding to the child so that the child's relationship to the school or home is developed and improved?

DK: I do not say anything to the child, nor to the adult. What is happening is something Jung describes as 'synchronicity'. Synchronicity is a coming together of an inner and an outer event or happening. When the children play here, they play an inner event. Since it is something which they have never done before it is a creation that comes from within. Now, here I am outside and I understand what is happening within the child. I participate in this happening because I understand what is going on through the symbols that the children use. This coming together of the inner and outer is a synchronistic event. And this is the basis for the next step without talking about it.

CT: What is the difference between the child playing in the garden with figures and playing here? What is going to make the difference?

DK: This room is what I call the free and protected space. The free and protected space means that this room is under my influence, my protection. So the children feel free to do whatever they want. They have to feel protected because when there is complete freedom they go beyond their boundaries. So what I have to pay attention to is how the child limits himself or herself when they play here and this has to be observed by what they use. Now we are coming into difficult fields.

CT:　What you are implying is that the ordinary classroom isn't appearing to the child as a free and protected space.

DK:　No, of course not.

CT:　And so the classroom atmosphere is hindering his or her development?

DK:　Hindering. Yes. There are a lot of demands in the classroom. I have found important what Jung described as the individuation process. Individuation refers to the development of the child as he or she becomes more and more conscious of their potentials and their inner life. At the same time the healing side of the psyche is also awakened. The psyche's development and its potential are hindered, as they are in the schools, by imposing demands on children in order to make them study or do whatever. If the psyche is let free, the healing capacity of the psyche takes over and guides the whole process.

CT:　So some of the pressure in the psyche of the child begins to break up and that allows spontaneous expression, free expression and this is the individuation?

DK:　No. This breaking up awakens the individuation. It's not yet happened. It must develop. The child can say whatever he or she likes but I would never ask anything. It is quite different from other therapies. Here nobody can actually understand what is happening. This is really the freedom of the psyche to work according to its nature. It is completely different from normal psychology.

CT:　But what about people like R.D. Laing and other psychiatrists who emphasise how important the influence of the parents and others are in shaping the behaviour of the child. Do you find it necessary to communicate with the parents or teachers? Can they, in fact, be working against you or against the child?

DK:　They could. But the first thing I do is to talk with the parents before I take the child. They can tell me all their complaints and whatever else they have to say about the child and I tell them how I will work with the child.

CT:　So you have to feel clear in yourself about your relationship to the parents.

DK: They can tell me all they are worried about. They give their worries to me and then I say to them, 'Now I take over. Feel free to let your child be here.' I tell the parents that sometimes the child's condition may be worse for a period. So I tell them beforehand that if it is too hard to deal with the child then they should telephone me and we can talk about it a little bit. I don't give them any other advice because otherwise the free and protected space for the child is broken. That might be difficult to understand. While the child is here, they talk. They can tell me stories or tell me what they are doing. That's fine but I would never explain anything to them. If they are having difficulties at school I might ask, 'Is it very difficult at school?' Usually they don't want to talk about it because this immediately goes on a different level. You see the work here has two basic elements, earth and water, and they are located in the body. So when you start to work you don't explain from the intellect. That would be a jump from one level to another; that would not work. We have to allow for the possibility for these two elements to express themselves.

CT: Obviously one is working on a much deeper level if the rational is being left behind.

DK: Yes, you then penetrate into deeper and deeper levels. If I don't talk then I can see much more. If I talked the interpretation would interfere with what is going to be shown. If the child is having difficulties they may exist on a certain level. It is shown from the point of view of the elements. We can see that when it goes beyond the elements, there may be peace. So the difficulties are only on a certain level which has an influence on the behaviour of the child. We don't think of that child as sick or not well. The main structure may be completely in order. What we hope to reach is the location of what Jung calls the 'Self'.

CT: What do you mean by 'the main structure?'

DK: The main structure of the whole personality is contained in the 'Self'. Jung calls the 'Self' the centre of the totality of the personality. That includes both the unconscious side and the conscious side. In Buddhism it would be called 'seeing the true nature arising'. This then becomes the basis of a transformation of energies. That is the amazing thing. So that all that has been against the child may begin to transform into constructive energies.

CT: For the child, the constructive energies would manifest in school as a mind that concentrates . . . Since you have now been in this work for some thirty years, have the behavioural patterns and problems of children changed very much in three decades?

DK: Oh yes, the problems have changed. It is becoming more and more difficult for children because the direction that the school takes is purely intellectual. Schools are leaving aside the creative within children, the expression of love and all those beautiful aspects of a young human being. When I started there was no television or very little. So when the child used African or Chinese figures it was purely archetypal. They hadn't seen anyone like that. Now the children see all these films and cartoons about monsters and when they come here, many choose monsters. We have to see what the monsters mean to the psyche of the child in comparison to what it was like for children before television.

CT: So you are saying that both the pressures in the school and the presence of television are having a major influence on the psyche of the child?

DK: Yes. A distortion of a complete aspect of the psyche is taking place.

CT: In other words children in school are often very passive except for the stimulation of the intellect, and at home passive due to sitting in front of the television. So the child's unconscious life is not getting a full and active expression.

DK: They push all those energies into the unconscious, all the feelings and the creativity. Feelings become unimportant. It's terrible. What we have now in the world is aggression which comes from this pressure. One day it has to explode. It is like a glass that is full of water. It is going to overflow. And this is shown more and more. I have to deal with these energies in the sand. Today the children want to make a fire, they want to make volcanoes, they want to make big explosions.

CT: In your contact with and relationship to children you are seeing something of a macroscopic view of children's life.

DK: Yes. Someone said, 'Kalff has the whole cosmos in her sand-pit.' It's true. It's there in the sandtray because all levels can be followed incredibly. The Dalai Lama has been here in this room. And when he was here he asked me why I have all these figures. I said maybe we have had a previous life and have lived in a different country. I have figures from different cultures so that many levels of the unconscious can be exposed.

CT: I would like to make a switch from children to adults. What are some of the differences you might find in an adult coming into this free and protected space?

DK: It is the same, really. When you come here you will be hesitant and say, 'Oh, my God, all these figures, what shall I do?' That is the first thing. So I have to make you comfortable and feel completely accepted. This is a very difficult task. We are so used to judging people. 'He is tall.' 'He is small.' 'He goes first with his left foot and what does that mean?' We are trained to do this and we must forget all about this. At school we studied Dr T.D. Suzuki, and he said, the first thing you have to do is to leave aside all you have learnt. This is something we have to do here. When you just accept what comes you feel comfortable. Then I say, 'Why don't you touch the sand?' Then you think that would be interesting and start.

CT: Within the diversity of figures that you have here, wouldn't a person think that one figure might represent different archetypes?

DK: That is a very good question. In Freudian psychology a stem means a penis and is always the same; it is fixed. Jung said that when a person uses one of these symbols you have to know at which moment the person uses that symbol and why. And then see which interpretation of the symbol is correct. So a Jungian therapist never says this always means this. I can only appraise the symbols through the sequence of the images that you choose. Jung said you never interpret one dream. You have to see what was before that and then look what comes after; then maybe you can tell what this one dream means.

CT: In Buddhist language this is called 'dependent arising'. Everything is in relationship to something else.

DK: Yes, absolutely. It has to do with that.

CT: Jung, perhaps of all psychologists, is famous and known for his work with people's dreams. As a therapist working with adults and children how much do you actually focus on dream life?

DK: Usually I ask people to write down their dreams and bring them to me. Then I have to see whether what is happening in the sand is on the same level as the dreams, to see if they are connected or not. Sometimes we see that the dream life is on a different level from the sand. Sometimes, and you would hardly believe it, the sandplay is on a *deeper* level than the dream. So I have to interpret both and see how they work together. The dream may illuminate something for me, tell me something. It is easy to interpret a dream. But because I interpret it, the dream must be brought to the conscious level to talk about it. During the sandplay, I don't interpret, so this remains on a deeper level – you go very much into your inner world and this may remain on a deeper level. But very often one affects the other. The dream affects the sandplay or the sandplay affects the dream.

CT: I very rarely have dreams or recall dreams. A dream came last night. It must be weeks since I can recall a previous dream.

DK: Maybe because you were coming here.

CT: I think so. Would it be unskilful or inappropriate to use the dream as a format with regard to sandplay? If I began to play with the sand should I leave the dream behind?

DK: Usually I ask for the dream. When a person comes for the first time the initial dream tells a lot about your life or difficulties or aims or whatever. We look at that dream and we see whether the sequence of dreams that follow are similar to the initial dream and similar to the initial sandplay. We can take it as diagnostic. Sometimes it is indicated whether there will be a good sequence or whether it will be difficult. You can decide whether to begin with the dream or not.

CT: At this point I want to start with the sandplay.

DK: Maybe you would like to see what the sand is like. Just make yourself comfortable. Take the chair over there and touch the sand. You can feel that this sand is a little bit damp. See whether you like this on your hand and then go over and touch the sand that is dry. Move to the tray that has the kind of sand that you prefer. If you would like the sand to be wetter there is water there. You can pour water in it as much as you like.

CT: The texture of this damp sand feels very familiar. It feels like English beaches.

DK: Oh, that reminds you of an English beach.

CT: Yes.

DK: And you like the English beach.

CT: Yes, very much.

DK: So you feel very comfortable here?

CT: Right. [*A few minutes pass by in silence while I move the sand about in the tray. I push the sand away from the centre of the tray so that the bottom, blue in colour, is revealed and makes a circle. I feel connected with the sand and with what I am seeing. And I don't feel the need to alter anything.*]

DK: That is enough for you?

CT: It feels enough. It feels good.

DK: So you have a good feeling.

CT: A very good feeling inside.

DK: Do you get any association with what you experience in front of you. First you said it reminded you of the beach.

CT: The association is meditation.

DK: Yes?

CT: This [the centre of the tray free from sand] feels like going deep. This sand seems to be the obstructions to going deep. The walls of the tray are also blue like the centre so the going deep and the expansiveness is greater than the obstructions. This is what the tray is communicating to me as I look at it. Blue for me always represents infinity.

DK: Infinity?

CT: Yes.

DK: So this is absolutely what it is. You go into infinity. All around is also infinity. And so this is what we have to deal with. The next time you come we might see what comes up. Maybe we need many more images to see what the obstructions are. When we go as deep as these images indicate we find the true nature. From there maybe the obstructions will disappear. But we can build up new and constructive things will appear.

CT: I begin to see the relationship more clearly of the sand to the blue. Would it be useful in this moment for me to look at some of the figures and bring them to the sandtray?

DK: Well, you said this is enough for now, didn't you?

CT: Yes, I did.

DK: Yes, so I accept that and that's why I started to talk. So, naturally, if you come a second time you are inclined to use the figures. This is how sandplay works.

CT: In other words, my immediate response is a completion but then after a while my thought comes in.

DK: Yes, but now I'll do an unorthodox thing . . . Now would you like to take some figures?

CT: Yes.

DK: Go and see, take some.

CT: [*In the silence I stood in front of one section of the shelves with the countless figures. I allowed my whole body to relax and let my eyes slowly wander around the figures. When I felt a strong or distinct*

*feeling in my stomach area in connection with one figure I selected
that figure and placed it in the tray. I proceeded slowly taking several
minutes before placing them in the tray and before speaking again.*]

I have selected eight. A small Japanese figure. The peacock with the
wings fully expanded. A green leaf. A small statuette of Jesus with his
finger pointing to the sacred heart. A tree. A naval boat. A man with
an axe, possibly from Rajasthan, India, and a musician. All these
figures particularly stood out for me.

In a way, they are all associated with the sand, which represented
the obstacles, and the blue base which seemed to be infinity. The navy
boat very much belongs to the sand. The leaf, which I initially thought
was the bodhi leaf (from the tree of enlightenment) belongs to the
blue base. The peacock, as beauty, also belongs to this blue area.
Although I have a tremendous love and affection for Jesus it took
some time in looking at the statuette for a feeling response to come
through. It was the heart that made that response for me. Shall I tell
you what they remind me of?

DK: Yes, if you like.

CT: The first one I selected from all the figures, the Japanese figure
reminded me very playfully of my little daughter. The tree reminded
me of my love of the trees. The boat, this naval boat, was the one
symbol that brought me some feelings of pain. My initial reminder
was of the British invasion of the Falklands and all that war symbol-
izes for me. The image of the figure holding the axe seemed to me to be
a very positive image. The axe is a symbol of cutting through to this
blue base. And the musician is because I love music, all music.

DK: You love music?

CT: When you mentioned synchronicity I was reminded of a rock
star, Sting. He actually goes to a Jungian therapist in England. The
name of one of his albums is *Synchronicity*. To an extent, I associate
music with the world of the sand and the world of the deep. All eight
figures brought for me a feeling response deep down in my body and
all feel to be important for me.

DK: Do you think the figures are independent or do they communicate with each other?

CT: Good question. [*At this point in the therapy session, it had not
occurred to me that the way the figures were placed in the sand and
the direction they were facing was of significance. The figures were
placed in the sand roughly in a circle. It meant that different figures*

were facing each other. It gave me a sudden fresh awareness of what was revealing itself.]

I can see the beauty of the peacock and the uncivilized activity of the naval boat opposite. Yet there is a fundamental relationship there. At this level, here in my navel, I feel both peacock and boat are interrelated. If I think about them I would say, 'I like this. I don't like that.' But on a deeper level, I would say they belong to each other.

DK: In other words you feel that everything plays a role in your life?

CT: Yes, yes. When I look at these three (the man with the axe, Jesus and the leaf) I feel them in a religious way. With the peacock which represents beauty, I associate it with the feminine.

DK: The feminine.

CT: Yes. [*A few moments of silence.*] Nothing is coming from inside which I can add to this. Again it feels complete. Any comments, Mrs Kalff?

DK: I don't know if I should give an interpretation or not.

CT: Would that be too unorthodox?

DK: It is of course. I don't do that in the first sandplay.

CT: It would be very useful for me to see how much each figure does represent for me.

DK: Well, you chose this as the first little figure. You said it reminds you of your little daughter. This is a Japanese God, a protector of little children. They hang these by their beds.

CT: What do I have to learn from that?

DK: There are three religious figures and here is the protector. He protects the youth, the young energies. I would say that probably your female side needs protection because it is still young and innocent. It is located opposite the boat so this may cause trouble in the outside world.

CT: What will cause trouble?

DK: The child-like female side of you.

CT: In the outside world?

DK: Yes. The whole heart is open here [*pointing to the Jesus statuette*] but is also like Manjushri cutting with the sword to make clear. So this too wants to develop more consciousness about that, more clarity. Now the peacock, in Tibetan Buddhism for instance, means beauty. He unfolds his beauty and is often seen in connection with the alchemic process of opening up, coming to the goal of totality. But the peacock can also take in the poison and transform it into its own medicine. So here would be a possibility to work with this side of yourself. It is very interesting that here the musician and Jesus with an open heart are also in a diagonal. They would probably stand for love and compassion. These are Christian symbols and the others are Eastern symbols. I'm not sure how these are related.

CT: I would say a major theme of my life is to integrate Eastern spirituality into the Western social reality.

DK: Ah, I see. There you have it. That is what I was thinking. And here the peacock is opposite the tree. What did you say about the tree?

CT: First, as a monk, I lived in the forest. I also speak to preserve trees and work for trees.

DK: I also see it as a natural growth.

CT: Yes, that goes deeper. The boat is the most difficult one.

DK: That is the difficulty you have with the animal in yourself, the female quality in yourself. You may have to develop this in order to find the integration of Buddhism into Christianity. There is a difficulty because of the heritage of Christianity and the new coming in of Buddhism. You were not born as a Buddhist. I think that may cause some trouble sometimes. Your inner female quality may have to be developed more. When the intellect becomes autonomous then it becomes a one-sided principle. We have to support it and nourish it. I always say these days there is a terrific need for nourishing the intellectual side. And nourishment means, in the feminine, a feeling capacity. It is a compassionate capacity and a deep spiritual capacity, that comes from the body, from within.

CT: I will sit for a few seconds just to see if anything else comes . . . No, it feels very complete. Nothing to take away and nothing to add.

DK: If I speak of a prognosis, it feels complete. The inner infinity goes to the outer infinity. All is in between these two aspects and they have come together. The diagnosis here is positive.

CT: I feel, Mrs Kalff, that we have explored the various areas and I've touched on everything I came to ask you about sandplay. Thank you.

The 'mad' are eccentric

An interview with Fr Benedict Ramsden
Totnes, Devon, England

When Benedict Ramsden was in his early twenties he lived with his wife Lilah in a remote village hamlet in the middle of Oxfordshire, England. One evening he and his wife 'invited God to take over their home'. That night God was appointed landlord and they offered their home to Him for the use of anybody that came. The very next night, a sick, broken-down man who was totally soaked through from a rainstorm knocked on their front door and asked for shelter. Lilah told me that God had 'taken up their offer immediately. We couldn't believe it.'

That first knock on their door set the pattern for the next twenty-five years and probably for the rest of their lives. The suicidal, the schizophrenic, the abused, the beaten, the lonely, the violent and the fearful have taken refuge in the home of the Ramsdens. They have been brought by doctors, nurses, social workers and family members and friends of the distressed. Some of those who come to live with the Ramsdens have come straight from the mental hospital, or the clinic, or from the terror of a violent household. By one means or another they have found their way to the Ramsden house.

Benedict Ramsden attended Keble College at Oxford University where he studied theology. Afterwards, he became a priest in the Russian Orthodox Church. His journey to the Church began when he was just two years old during World War II. During the war many were sent from the city to stay with families in the countryside, where it was thought to be safer from Nazi bombs. An elderly woman stayed at the home of Benedict in Oxfordshire. She was a Russian Orthodox Christian and prayed daily before a lighted icon in her room. This was the first of a number of important contacts that he would have with the Orthodox Church.

After university, Benedict and his young family moved from Oxfordshire, where he had lived since he was born, to Willand in Devon. Once again, their home became a place of refuge where, at times, families in crisis would be sleeping on the living room floor. Not only did the Ramsdens take on a wide range of suffering adults and emotionally disturbed children but they also had eight children of their own. Today their children's ages range from nine years to twenty-seven.

In 1983, he, his wife and eight children moved to Totnes in South Devon. They persuaded a local bank manager to give them a mortgage on a seventeenth-century family house that was up for sale in the middle of the town, and again left their front door open. The local health authorities were quick to take advantage of their skills and the house was soon full. The Ramsdens have gained a reputation for being especially effective working with people classified as schizophrenic – not only reducing or eliminating their drug dependency but also enabling their guests to regain their sense of self-worth and value as human beings.

Throughout the years, Fr Benedict Ramsden, who is now 49, has been approached many times and commissioned on a number of occasions to write about the work he and his wife are involved in. However, the fullness of the day, which begins at six o'clock with a service, does not give him much opportunity for sitting at a desk. There are also four children remaining at home, by now well-adapted to the impact their parents' guests have on the household.

Our meeting was held in the drawing room of his beautiful, old house. The bookshelves are filled with large volumes on the Russian Orthodox Church, religious art, history and the works of William Blake. Classical records, icons, a television as well as a video and all the usual array of contemporary and antique furniture litter the spacious room.

After the meeting with him I returned to my car in the driveway. It was a cold, wet winter's night. The car was stuck between two other cars and a post and I was unable to move it. One of the Ramsdens' residents, a young man wearing only a cotton shirt, trousers and running shoes was walking around the garden. In a faltering voice, he asked me if he could be of assistance. He guided me as I steered the car forward and backwards a few inches at a time to squeeze out. It took several minutes by which time he was totally soaked, if not chilled to the bone. I thanked him. He shrugged his shoulders and continued his walk. I was left wondering whether a so-called mentally healthy person would have willingly gone to so much trouble on such a night.

CT: I would like to talk with you about how you are using your home. What is happening in your household?

BR: For about twenty years my wife and I, along with our eight children, have kept an open door to people who have wanted to live with us. Over the years and particularly for the past fifteen years or so, this has evolved into our caring for people with schizophrenia and related conditions in our home.

For a long time we just looked after anyone who came along. I don't think there was anything particularly wonderful about it. We were probably lonely and just liked letting people into our house. [*Smiling.*] Years ago we used to take in people of all sorts – homeless families, abused and battered children and people with mental difficulties. People who had schizoid tendencies, whatever they are, seemed to thrive with us. The result was a build up of pressure from various social agencies for us to take others.

'Mary did quite well with you, so would you like to try with Jane?' In that way the whole thing slowly grew more and more specialized. In a way that is a sad thing. The law was not terribly interested then and it was possible to mix everybody up in a way which would not be possible under the kind of regulations we have today. It is terribly difficult to bring all sorts of people together in one home.

CT: Where did your training skills come from?

BR: They are intuitive. I'm not a nurse, a doctor, a psychiatrist or psychologist. It would appear that my wife and I have a knack at handling a certain kind of person. Or probably we create an approach or space for a person to have the chance to do some flourishing.

In the past twenty years there has been a move in Britain towards community care of the mentally ill. For years and years they were buried in vast baronial mansions built in the last century about four miles out of towns and cities. Those places had a once beautiful name, 'asylum', which over the years was changed by those very places into something terrible. Then came a new idea, one with which I am in complete agreement. Instead of pushing the 'mad' out of society, perhaps the place to look after them is in it.

CT: What happened?

BR: Unfortunately, the implementation of this scheme coincided with a shortage of money as well as with a shortage of time because many things had been put off too long. One might even think, the way things have gone in some places, that the whole policy was created in order to save money. You can't push the so-called mentally ill into a community that cannot cope with them. You must first change the community and that takes a lot of time and deliberate policy of education and preparation.

People from Russia, for example, think our society is unspeakably shocking in the way we treat our old people. We herd them into special old people's ghettos – old peoples homes, and eventually, into hidden places, unmentionable and unfaceable places. In our culture no one wants to know about dying or death.

East Europeans are also shocked about the way we treat children. They just can't understand us. In many cultures, as probably once in England, the mad have been regarded as, perhaps, touched by something beyond our normal experience. They were treated almost with veneration. But for years our society has herded them out and hidden them.

We reject these people in a special way which we make look like kindness. We dress up what we are doing by giving it a much nicer name, so that for instance, banishing an old person to a ghetto for the senile is called 'giving them peace and quiet'. But it's really the British habit of euphemism at work. We call something by a nice name in order to pretend it doesn't exist. You may notice my use of the word 'mad'. I do so deliberately because it avoids a dangerous euphemism. There is a right way of using the expression 'mentally ill' and the model of a mental illness has its uses and its truth. The concept is dangerous when taken literally.

CT: Contemporary social thinking puts people into categories and fixes them in a particular way. What is your experience of people who are classified as mentally ill or schizophrenic?

BR: They display symptoms like hearing voices, having visions, feeling a control from outside, withdrawal from relationships, paranoia and so on. I don't intend to deny the reality of any of these symptoms or of a link between them. But I do wonder to what extent we should regard them as sick in themselves. For example, we talk about people who are labelled schizophrenic. This is a vague umbrella word we use when someone who has had a mental breakdown exhibits five or so out of about thirty different symptoms. Yet we use it as though it refers to something as specific as measles.

Of about one per cent of the population who break down, the symptoms are the same all over the globe. But in certain sorts of societies nearly all of that one per cent become disabled. Their lives become a total tragedy. Very significantly, in other societies the proportion of these same people with these same predisposing factors is much, much less. It is obvious that schizophrenic breakdown depends not only on factors in the patient but also on factors in the society around. In a highly competitive and demanding society, where everyone must prove his or her worth, breakdown is much more likely than in one where dignity is afforded a person simply because he or she exists. To have a schizophrenic personality in our sort of society is an almost certain damnation to catastrophe. For example, our society has very little time for people with artistic temperament, or for someone who isn't into making money. The fact is we need all sorts of human contributions to society.

CT: What is going to change the consciousness of people when the community is so competitive?

BR: We need to learn to accept others for what they are and not for what we think they ought to be, to accept what they can offer and not what we think they ought to offer. And we certainly won't learn to accept people unless we meet them. I moved into this house six years ago. At that time the law governing the activity that I am engaged in was so vague as to be almost non-existent. I bought this house and I just moved in with a rather large group of people. No one in the street took a great deal of notice, though it must have been obvious that a few of these people were perhaps a little bit odd at times.

Two or three years ago vast mental institutions were closed and people were dumped on an exploitive market. So parliament passed legislation aimed to give local authorities a weapon to clobber people who were exploiting the unfortunate by packing five into a room in order to get money from the state. So the new law said that a house with three people or more in it who had at any time been mental patients had to be registered as an institution. So I had to apply for planning permission to register.

Usually in such circumstances the neighbours hit the roof. 'Good God, they are going to open up a lunatic asylum next door to my house! The value of my property will slump!' In my case, they were reassured that all I was doing was getting retrospective permission to do what I was already doing. Then most of the people in the street sent letters of support for my planning application. Our neighbours had ceased to think of 'schizophrenics' and thought instead of people as themselves, the individuals they knew, not as members of any category but as persons. Now that outcome is an unusual situation. Normally you hit an enormous wave of opposition.

I haven't taken people out of a big lunatic asylum and built some modern little lunatic asylum in the middle of the street. I'm just living my own life with my family in our own house and sharing it with other human beings. Our guests may have certificates to say they are dotty. In fact, they are not all that much dottier than me. No one stops to think that these people have in the past been locked up in high security units at the cost of nearly £1000 a week.

CT: Isn't it dangerous for you and your family to befriend these 'eccentric' people?

BR: The people I have here need a bridge back to society. This is an alternative to the madhouse, the lockup. I have people who were in very high security situations indeed. They are brought into this house, some of them having just come, quite literally, from locked cells. They are let into this house with everything that's here to be thrown around. It's obvious that there are dozens of things around the house that can be used as a weapon for attack, that there are precious things which can be broken. The moment they walk into this room they are at once impressed by someone having a totally different set of expectations of them. There are no straps, no pads, no heavies or hypodermics at the ready and the room hasn't been cleared of possible weapons. They walk into a beautiful English drawing room which contains some beautiful things. Not only are they being met with trust, to them it seems like a princely sort of room and they are being treated like aristocrats.

CT: Atmosphere can't protect you and your family from latent patterns of violence and suicide? How do you deal with that?

BR: I can only say that no one has ever hurt me. I'm the most awful coward. I couldn't do this if I really thought I was going to get hurt. In whatever way I tackle the aggression that crops up it is not going to be by a head-on show of strength. I might get hurt!

And then I've got children. Most of my younger children have grown from babyhood with this work going on around them. They too have not been hurt.

When someone comes into this room they see there are several things to throw around. I'm giving into their hands the power to hurt me. Because they have that power given them, they do not need to seize it. I also give them the right to be angry. I think that anger is a proper part of human make-up. If you really hold anger down you are heading for trouble and likely blow-ups. Human beings must have space and opportunity to be angry.

For instance, I had a young man who came here. Just a few days before he came it took five men to remove him from where he was and most of them were hurt, some quite badly hurt in the struggle, and these men were heavies, the sort you use as bouncers in a night club. They were the bouncers for society. Now I had read that young man's history and I regarded that young man's anger as legitimate, so I gave him the opportunity to express it.

CT: In what way?

BR: If he was really angry, my wife or I would simply join in with him and do whatever he was doing, shake with him or struggle with him or just cuddle him. We would say, 'Of course, you are angry.' We would take him somewhere where he could have a good scream or we would go caving together [*a journey to some nearby caves*]. There he could go through some deep experience like fear or anger. If I was feeling really brave I might have a wrestle with him.

There is a lot of aggression and competitiveness in people which can be converted into play. In fact it is in play that most of us learned how to handle our aggression. I'm not talking about games like playing cricket with its highly ritualized structures, but about much simpler levels of play like arm wrestling or Cowboys and Indians or just tousling about on the lawn. But people can't handle it when it's linked with anger. People won't get into those situations with 'dangerous people' because they are frightened of getting hurt. If you go into those sorts of situations and regard it as a game then the person isn't presented with *your* fear and anger. Then you get some very different results.

CT: Doesn't this require total acceptance of the person?

BR: I wouldn't say total. My acceptance is extremely imperfect. But they are more than willing to accept me on the same terms that I accept them. I accept them as they are and I don't pretend that I am not a mess myself. Perhaps I am prepared to be more accepting than some people are. Even then I show them that my acceptance is a mess, too. The person can feel that he or she belongs here and has a right to be here. It is quite rightfully not a peaceful situation. This is a place where you can bring your anger and your lack of peace. You can shout about it, swear about it, beat your fists on the ground or talk about it if you want to. That evaporates a lot of the violence that surrounds it. I think it is an unhealthy suppression of anger which makes us violent. What is important is coming to terms with the fact that we, with all our frustrations and with all the anger that stems from them, have a right to be here.

CT: Here on Earth, here in life.

BR: Yes, here in existence. You don't qualify for being here by being accepted by others, by matching up to some model of behaviour, however generous that model. The whole of existence is an extraordinary mystery . . . or a meaningless nonsense; that's a possibility that we all live with. But even then, it is a chaos out of which the most extraordinary visions of order can come from time to time.

I happen to believe there is a little more than chaos to it. I believe that every human being is some unique vision of something significant. I don't know what that something significant is. I think you have to meet people as they are without trying to impose on them your understanding of what they are. Then people don't feel threatened in their very existence. I think metaphysics is nearer to the surface in people than we imagine. Something so precious is perceived as being forced into a stereotype and so the person instinctively reacts. When a person sees clearly that he doesn't fit into the stereotype, and that people are going to bring all sorts of force to make him do so, even to the point of cells and straps and drugs, I'm not surprised that violence is sometimes the outcome.

CT: What takes place when a person has left the institution and he or she walks through your front door to meet you and the family for the first time?

BR: Nothing very dramatic. The very first thing that happens is a slightly middle class reception. Someone brings tea, coffee and biscuits. We all sit around on the sofas in this beautiful room. It is all a bit stilted. I'm painfully shy and very conscious of the experts who have come with the new arrivals. I am very aware of their curiosity about how I am going to handle things and so I get more and more inhibited.

The nurses, social workers and doctors go away and we start doing things without thinking. We'll probably just pile into the kitchen and get the next meal, involving the new arrival at whatever level he or she can be involved. We would certainly bring them into something ordinary and something with an element of enjoyment in it. For example, the day after the violent person I just spoke about came, we went caving. Some people thought it was a bizarre thing to do with him. The caves are about six miles from here in Buckfastleigh. We went through a series of caves used by the Royal Marines to test men for personal selection. The course is said to quite often reduce the average Marine to tears. At the other end of the cave the Marine might come out shattered. For the first time in his life he has perhaps been underground and got really frightened through being stuck here and there for a few minutes. He finally comes out with a surge of adrenalin and sheer relief and excitement and he splashes around in the icy river to wash the mud off. My lot have just done the same and no one can tell the difference. Royal Marines and lunatics look exactly the same! And I'm not making a cynical point.

CT: That experience would dissolve differences.

BR: There is a parallel to that in the home. Homes aren't places of tranquility. You know a family is a pretty abrasive atmosphere for growing. We don't run some marvellous saintly vision of the way a Christian home ought to be or something like that. If my wife and I are going to have a row, we've learned long ago how good it is to have a row in front of the people we look after; let them see that the world isn't divided into two classes, the professionals who wear white coats and sit behind desks and never have emotions, and the 'mad' who have all the emotions. Anger wells up from time to time between my wife and me and this is part of how the real world is. For some of the guests here, this is an extraordinary recognition. Some of the people that come to me have been in a mental hospital since childhood.

One woman here had been in the hospital between the ages of nine and twenty-three. All the emotion she would have seen, except for some exasperation from the staff, would have been regarded as 'mad'. It is for her an extraordinary experience to see ordinary people's rows and their emotions, and then the patching up and the forgiveness and the carrying on of the relationship. What we are doing here is so ordinary that there's hardly anything to say about it. We are letting back into ordinary life people who for some very odd reason have been pushed right out of ordinary life by our society.

CT: How many people come to stay here at a time?

BR: We look after a total of eleven people, some in this house and some in another house run by friends of ours who are trying to repeat our methods. Years ago the Social Services would ring us up late at night and say, 'We've got a homeless family. Put them up on your floor or we'll have to split them up.' The house was crawling with people. It was enormous fun. Now the law has changed and one wouldn't be allowed to live in such a lovely way.

CT: What is the result of closing down the mental hospitals and sending people back into society?

BR: I've watched it go all wrong. It is a national disgrace. People are committing suicide all over the place. Having spent up to sixty years in a secure surrounding with constant room temperature of 70 degrees and three meals a day arriving punctually, they are then thrown out into some bed and breakfast in some lonely doss house. People are killing themselves or dying of trauma. It is an appalling national disaster and no one wants to know about it because we don't concern ourselves with the 'mad'. Certainly asylums are misused, underfunded and understaffed. But there are some people who need shelter, need an asylum in the best sense of this beautiful word. But in the midst of all this disaster I have also watched, at first hand, a lot of people who have gained tremendously from being integrated into the community.

CT: What about the homes being built for those coming out of incarceration in a hospital?

BR: The authorities so often build a little community project to house the mentally ill costing a million pounds or more, and staffed with a team of professionals. Yet it is built so much on the model of the old one that there is no breakthrough into a new understanding. It is simply a mini-lunatic asylum in the middle of the town instead of a maxi one outside it. Oddly enough, because it is small there is sometimes even less room for humanity. At least in a big institution there are usually places to skive off into and be human.

Because I have a religious label some people assume we are working some kind of white magic or spiritual healing or that we have some peculiar gift. They can then dismiss us as an exception. Recently we decided to repeat what is going on here. We set up another house with a couple who said they were willing to let people into their home. Most of it is intuitive and it really takes a conscious intellectual effort to describe what we actually do. Our methods, so far as they can be said to be methods, are being repeated there and are producing the same results.

CT: People come here to stay and experience a normal household. Isn't there a reluctance for people to leave? Don't you have a stable population?

BR: People come here first of all on an experimental footing. That isn't determined by time. Eventually there comes a mutually recognised time when they say they want this to be their home and when we say that is okay with us. Then they have more or less the same rights as our own children. No one wants their children to hang around their necks until they are senile. But if you want them to go away, first they must be secure. Once secure they can take risks and leap off. We make this commitment that if you go away, even if it's after a blazing row, you can always come back here. You may not leave in some ideal state – 'Brother, you are cured. This is the great day that we wave you off.' You may be a mess when you go away. But whatever terms you go away on, you may always come back. The place is not locked up. You can let yourself in, help yourself to some food, find a bed or mattress. The house belongs to you.

CT: Doesn't that get abused?

BR: It gets abused sometimes. Sometimes people decide that this is just a place of asylum and all they want to do is stay here. To a certain extent that is all right, but obviously we hope for more. The world out there is pretty rough and painful. But there are a lot of attractions and once people have the confidence, these draw them out of the parental home. It is restrictive to live in a parental home with big daddy and big mama. We've got our style and that inevitably cramps the style of our children and everybody that lives with us. There is the great draw of girlfriends and boyfriends in the world out there. It is no use to give them six months to build themselves a bridge to the outside world. It would be like being sentenced to death. A child will leave when he or she has the confidence because the world out there is seen as enjoyable.

CT: So is confidence the key?

BR: Perhaps the key is enjoyment. One of the really heavy things about our society is that it doesn't believe in enjoyment. It doesn't believe in joy. Although it pretends to, it doesn't believe in pleasure. We really do think there is something questionable about it. And certainly the mad are not entitled to enjoy themselves.

CT: What is the difference between joy and pleasure? Isn't the primary interest for millions the pursuit of pleasure?

BR: In trying to make a distinction I don't wish to imply any rejection of pleasure. By joy, I suppose I mean those kinds of happiness that understand even misery. That's joy – when you can march happily into the mouth of a lion. And it starts with the simplest pleasures. Every step of joy is a step in the direction of something utterly profound which makes the courage to exist possible. So right from the start we encourage people here to enjoy themselves. Joy draws you out beyond the limits of what you are in. So here I am trying, through enjoyment, to point the way to a much larger vision.

CT: There are no visible symbols of religion here.

BR: You are wrong. There are icons all around. There is quite a big one, called 'Joy Unexpected', as you walked in. You are making a point though. While Christianity is not concealed, it is not pushed at you. You don't get a lot of God talk in this house. For one thing a lot of people who have come here have latched on to God talk as the language of their madness. Take for instance this symptom of being controlled by external forces. For some people such hallucinatory forces are seen as God or angels or, of course, devils. God language and popular religion is so damaged by puritanism and so bound up with guilt that it has actually become dangerous, particularly for many of those who come to be with us.

Some, for example, have never adjusted to the discovery of their physicality and, in particular, their sexuality. They are not able to love themselves and accept themselves in that sort of way. When that is linked up with morbid guilt and popular puritanism, then God talk becomes extremely damaging. I think there is too much God language around already and one forgets it is a very inadequate language that tries to give sound to silence.

CT: Do you have any kind of ritual or services here? Do you dress as an orthodox priest?

BR: I dress most of the time in ordinary clothes. But not always. If I'm going to be in a situation where it is appropriate, I dress in the traditional dress of a priest. I do it much more naturally than I would, say, dress for dinner, and I don't regard it in any way as embarrassing or disturbing. There is a chapel at the heart of the house. Services are held there at six o'clock in the morning. If anyone wants to come they have to get out of bed. There is no reward for coming. If people come to the services to get approval from us, they soon discover things don't work here in that way. There also isn't a pressure to keep people away. If it were one side or the other, I would lean slightly towards discouraging people simply because of the dangers for some.

CT: What does 'spiritual' mean for you?

BR: It describes the fundamental resource for me to lead a life in which I'm not afraid of what most people are afraid of. There is some kind of peace here, in the middle of something very chaotic, which can be communicated by a kind of silence. You can live, have fun, fool around and still convey that you are rejoicing in your existence, which is perhaps the most fundamental thing a religious person does.

CT: So out of the silence comes rejoicing, enjoyment and play.

BR: And also forgiveness. Forgiveness has got linked up with guilt and being 'let off', rather than with love and being allowed to 'grow up'. I think forgiveness happens before you do wrong rather than afterwards. In an odd way we have the right to be wrong. Children in their own home have the right to be naughty because being naughty is part of growing up.

Acceptance is to allow people to exist in their own existence. Forgiveness is something like that. We could have an argument, of course, as to where forgiveness stops and sheer condoning of evil begins. Forgiveness is some sort of generosity that allows people their mistakes, their failures and their dignity; and with God that generosity is infinite.

CT: In the process of growing up, children are quite often self-conscious, especially when bringing friends home. Have any of your children said, 'Look, Mum and Dad, do we have to have these people with us all the time?' Have they been accepting, if not forgiving, of your open house policy?

BR: Of course they have. Any child who survives their childhood is only able to do so because they have learnt forgiving. I can say that there has been very little negativity. My grown up children, like all children, will occasionally complain about their childhood. Parents must expect to be clobbered with what they've done to their children. But mostly my children say they didn't realize how extraordinary their life was until they went to the homes of other children which, they say, seemed very boring compared to their own. My children have a fund of the most extraordinary stories.

I remember my teenage son bringing home a new girlfriend. At the time we had someone living with us who was very disturbed and had a habit of wailing and screaming. She used to think that the house had become a ship which was sinking. And she would run her fingernails down doors. She didn't open the doors but just liked to scrape behind them. My son was making his girlfriend coffee late at night in the kitchen. Behind the door there was this extraordinary howling and scratching going on which my son treated as though it wasn't there. It was like in *Jane Eyre*, where Mr Rochester's mad wife is kept in the East Wing. There in our kitchen sat this poor girlfriend, with eyes as big as saucers, not quite daring to ask, and my son didn't explain it for hours. We thought it was awfully mean but he thought it was rather funny.

All sorts of other 'mad' things go on in our home. (I'm allowing here for the word to be used in all sorts of nice ways.) Living in this mad house has enriched our lives and for the most part our children will say the same for themselves too. One or two very old people have died here and that too has been enriching, and the children have mourned their loss as much as my wife and I.

CT: Have your children missed out on anything?

BR: They have missed out on some of the orderly quietness of average suburban life. But then they have also missed out on much of the tedium. I would say one thing my children are not frightened of is mental illness in themselves or others. They have met madness and death and so they do not go around in a state of dread, wondering what these things would be like if they were to turn up.

CT: What would you say to someone who genuinely wishes to explore ways and means to accommodate people in the fringes of the mainstream of society?

BR: I'd say, please do. In our case we learnt as we went along. One has to purify one's motivation as one goes along. I thing that especially one must be very wary of picking up vulnerable people in order to boost one's own lack of inner security.

CT: What kind of people are suitable to house eccentric people?

BR: Well, I'm very struck by the fact that I live in a town with a hippyish element. I know it is an old-fashioned word to use. I have eleven people who are helping me with this work and nearly all of them have this alternative element about them. Now a lot of alternative people don't fit into the work structures of ordinary society. They get pushed to the fringes of it and aren't much valued. It offers them not much more than the dole. Yet these people, who are not interested in a highly competitive way of living, often have a kind of laid-backness which could be opened out into a welcoming attitude that is needed for fostering. Economically, this would be marvellous because of the real saving in pounds and pennies to the community. The savings in terms of human happiness would be extraordinary.

CT: Why doesn't this happen?

BR: Because it involves risk, and one of the ways we justify excluding the vulnerable from society is by claiming that we are protecting them from risk. It will only happen when society is willing to face these rejected people. We have to learn to take risks with them just as we take risks with our own children and so-called 'normal' human beings. Inevitably there would be a few mistakes but truly this is a way forward. What I would like to see is a sort of fostering scheme in which there are people with no remarkable skills but who have an ordinary level of acceptance of humanity. What we are doing is something like that and it isn't really anything remarkable. It could be repeated a thousand times over. When you think of those whacking great hospitals that held four to five thousand people all closing down and almost nothing to put in their place and then look at the sheer waste of these non-competitive people, many of them could do such a lot of healing.

CT: Thank you, Father Ramsden.

The field of mythology

An interview with Ram Dass
Barre, Massachusetts, USA

In the early 1960s, Richard Alpert was regarded by his peers as being a bright Jewish intellectual all set to reach the top of the academic ladder. That was until he swallowed his first psychedelic tablet. In social terms, it cost him dearly. He was a professor of psychology at the University of Harvard, Cambridge, Massachusetts, one of the two most prestigious North American universities; and he was asked to leave. He left in 1963 and was barred from the American Psychology Association. For the next four years he was a proponent of psychedelics and the older generation was up in arms.

He soon realised that though psychedelics got the user high, he or she didn't say there. 'It was clear you had to do something else to become what you could taste was possible,' he told me.

In 1967 Richard Alpert travelled to Iran, Pakistan, Nepal and India. 'I finally ended up at the feet of my guru, Neem Karoli Baba,' he says. (Neem Karoli is the name of a railway station in India. The name of the guru refers to the spiritual brother, *baba*, who lives near the railway station!) He was given the name Ram Dass, which meant Servant of God.

After practising hatha yoga, raja yoga and studying the *Bhagavad Gita*, he wrote *Be Here Now*, which has sold a million copies and gave Ram Dass worldwide recognition. He has made a number of return visits to India.

In 1973, he initiated the Hanuman Foundation which has given birth to many worthwhile projects, such as the Prison Ashram Project, which includes a massive correspondence programme connecting people who are in prison with people in the outside world. The Foundation has also sponsored projects and workshops for the dying and their families and friends. Over the years, thousands of people facing death have received love, support and honest counselling through these workshops.

In more recent years, Ram Dass formed the Seva Foundation, which serves as a vehicle for compassionate action around the world. Primarily, the Foundation has taken on the gigantic task of ending blindness in Nepal. Through fund raising in the United States,

American doctors have been flying into Nepal to save the eyesight of countless Nepalese. It is estimated that just £10 will save a child or adult from blindness. The Foundation also encourages self-employment of American Indians by promoting their arts and crafts. They experience one of the highest rates of unemployment in the Western world.

During the years, his books have reached a wide audience in the West. Others include *Grist for the Mill, The Only Dance There is, Journey of Awakening, Miracle of Love* and his latest book, *How Can I Help?*, co-authored with Paul Gorman.

Throughout the years he has spoken to massive audiences in the United States. I once went to listen to him in a college hall in Cape Cod on the coast of Massachusetts. More than a thousand people filled the auditorium. Ram Dass was greeted like a celebrity. He sat crossed-legged on a backless chair and for the next three hours touched upon every conceivable aspect of spiritual life, including devotion, service, knowledge, action and religious experiences. He loves relating his personal stories from the East and West and never appears to tire of telling the same one about himself he has told on countless occasions. He is thought-provoking, exceptionally eclectic – being very supportive of the variety of spiritual practices and therapies – and very funny. He is known for his immense and sustained devotion to his guru, and his work in the service of God.

On one lecture tour, which took place over a period of two months, he spoke to more than 100,000 people. Through his tours, he has raised money for the foundations while providing people of all ages and backgrounds with the opportunity to examine the quality of their lives.

I met with Ram Dass at the Insight Meditation Society in Barre, Massachusetts, where he was spending six weeks in meditation. To his credit, Ram Dass has not rested upon his laurels. He continues to participate in workshops and retreats given by other teachers both in the East and in the West. Despite being one of the most charismatic and public figures in spirituality, he continues to make himself and his personal life accessible to people, warts and all.

We agreed upon a 45-minute meeting for the interview. In fact, it ran for three hours. He is very personable and very engaging. In the beginning of the interview there is a touch of humour which features in his communications.

The interview begins with Ram Dass talking about the time when he returned from India. He was the first of my interviews, recorded when Cold War feelings were at their most intense.

CT: What happened when you came back from India in 1968?

RD: I continued teaching which at this time was an amalgam of my
training as a psychologist, my involvement with meditation, Hindu-
ism and drugs. I had to keep on listening to how they all fit in. I didn't
want to go back to the role I played with the drug scene in the sixties.

One day while I was spending time at my father's farm, I went to
town in my father's big car and some young hippies came up to me on
the street and said, 'Are you the connection that came up from Boston
with the acid?' I said, 'No, I'm not that kind of connection for you.' I
invited them to visit the farm and they brought their friends. Then
they invited their parents and their parents brought their ministers.
Soon there were 300 people dropping in on a weekend just to sit
around and talk dharma under the tree. Some of them wanted to stay
around so my dad said they could stay up on the hill. We had a
community of about ninety people living in tree houses and tents with
a meditation hall that we built.

After that I started to lecture around the country. My first lectures
would last up to eight or nine hours. In 1971 I went back to India to
be with Maharaj-ji [Neem Karoli Baba]. He said to me, 'No ashrams,
no monasteries,' which has saved me from being in the hotel business
many times! In the seventies, spirituality became very big. It became
attractive to the upper middle class, primarily Jewish and Protestant.
They were very comfortable with their affluence but somewhat
dispassionate about it. After some time, people began to realize that,
though they could taste the spiritual possibilities, it was going to take
effort and patience to realign their lives. The West is not noted for its
patience.

The fad started to pass in the late 1970s and the numbers started to
go down for the most part. The Buddhist tradition began attracting
the very intelligent and committed but for many others the fad came
and went because their level of devotion was too superficial.

CT: What about the overall interest today?

RD: After the Vietnam involvement there was a lot of despair about
political action. A lot of people were looking for things to do outside
the mainstream of society, so they came to spiritual things. Now once
again there is a kind of idealistic involvement in social-political
action. It is a spin-off from the fear about nuclear energy and nuclear
weapons. There is also a cynical materialism, which has given rise to
the 'yuppies' – which are the young upwardly-mobile people. It is

materialism with a vengeance. Economic insecurity affects whether people turn inward or not.

Older people are showing much more interest in spiritual awakening after having finished most of their working life. This seems to stem out of having gone through many life experiences already. They are more mature. I'm quite interested in working with 40, 50, 60 year old people. This is partly because of my age. I am 53. I am interested in the elders of society and how we can honour them and how they can honour themselves. For the most part, we have knowledgeable people in our society but not wise people.

The elderly are often rejected and put out to pasture. Since I'm still outside the establishment, I have been working with rejected groups for a number of years. They are not going to give me their children to work with, so I work with prisoners and the dying and now with older people.

CT: In a way you are in a rather unusual position. You have one foot well-grounded with the establishment and the other with the non-establishment.

RD: You are exactly right. Being an ex-druggie makes me accessible to a whole section of society; I've been to the East which makes me accessible to another section; I've got a Ph.D. in psychology and I was a Harvard professor, that makes me accessible to another section; I am bisexual and there is a whole segment who love me because I am one of them.

CT: So you are in touch with your peers.

RD: For the last twenty years I have had very little peer relationship at all except for a few my age like Allen Ginsberg [the poet] and Alan Watts [late writer on Zen]. Now I am beginning to be with peers.

CT: What is your view on the teachers who are coming from the East?

RD: Christopher, you've been in the East as I have. We know what a 'real' teacher is. From my point of view, 'real' teachers can do anything they want to do because they are 'real' teachers. What we have now in the West is not necessarily the cream of the crop. The teachers who came to the West often wanted something on the personal level. There was a tendency in the 1970s to elevate anybody who came along and say they were a guru and then project onto them. We were building them up to cut them down. This is what we often do with our politicians. It is almost like a ritual sacrifice. We give them a year or so of power and then burn them.

So many teachers see themselves as bearers of the truth, the truth that will set people free, and everything else is some sort of bastardization of that. The ego gets involved. The teacher has a vested interest in transmitting something. They are not interested in the peace and harmony of the world. They see that as a very short-term thing. They see the world as a place of suffering and they want to give birth to a method that will last. They want their students to be preoccupied with the lineage, so they don't lose it the minute he dies. It's a hard job, a damn hard job.

If a teacher is transmitting a lineage and you go in with a pure heart you can receive the teachings rather than the lineage. You can get the teachings and they get their own impurities. You don't have to worry about *their* impurities. They have to do their own work. All this can do is force people to trust their hearts more. You go for the teachings rather than the teacher, and you see teachers as teachings, rather than as teachers.

CT: If the emphasis is on maintaining the tradition and the methodology, mixing with global realities would certainly be watering it down, but if it is encouraging the spirit to come out . . .

RD: I understand. Then the question is: Where is the practice in relation to the spirit? Is the teacher responsible for the transmission of a lineage of practice, or for the touching and emerging of the spirit?

CT: Exactly.

RD: That is interesting. I'm in the spirit business! I'm not a Hindu. I'm only interested in spirit.

CT: The way you were speaking before, you sounded more sympathetic to the transmission of lineage than the transmission of the spirit.

RD: What I am saying is that the staying power of spirit is in part dependent on the input from rigorous practices.

CT: Do you see yourself as a transmitter of the lineage stemming from your guru? This lineage may have handed teachings from guru to disciple for generations. Are you the successor?

RD: The predicament is that it is very hard to enunciate that lineage. It has no form. He would say, 'Meditate!' and then he would disturb you and laugh at you when you meditated. It is the form of love and service, I guess. It's a peculiar system to transmit. He said to me, 'Go, do it!' but he didn't give me any tools except to love everyone, serve everyone and remember God. I realized by the middle seventies that in some way I was going to have to embrace worldly life in order to be free and embrace my humanity, whatever that meant.

CT: You then began to get more involved politically?

RD: I saw that every time I got involved in political action, things rose up in me that made me feel so useless – in the sense of being able to do something to bring the end of suffering – that I would retreat back. I wasn't ready. But now I see that was my work. Christ speaks of 'being in the world but not of the world.' I saw that I now had to be *in* the world in the sense of honouring the various identities, such as being a member of a family, a nation, an ecosystem, a species, a religion, etc.

CT: You were getting encouragement to get involved?

RD: Allen Ginsberg kept encouraging me. I had been thinking at the time, 'When Maharaj-ji wants me to do this, it will feel intuitively right.' And it was beginning to. For example, about three years ago, I was in Boulder to give a lecture and I got a call from Allen in New York. There was going to be a demonstration at Rocky Flats which is a big nuclear centre near Boulder. The Buddhists were going to have a meditation out there. He was supposed to be the front person for it but he couldn't go. Could I go in his place? So I found myself sitting on a zafu [meditation cushion] meditating in the middle of this scene, feeling like I was in the right place at the right moment.

Another example. A couple of years ago I decided to enjoy my humanity. I was in San Francisco, sort of hiding out. I didn't want to be Ram Dass. A minister of a church asked me to be his guest on a Sunday morning and speak from the pulpit. I had never spoken from a pulpit before, so I agreed. He mentioned a date which I forgot about. Now I'm in San Francisco cavorting about and I get this message that he is expecting me on Sunday morning. I was up all Saturday night and now I'm hung over. I want to be asleep, but I go to this church. It turns out it was Peace Day at the church. The Buddhist monks who are walking around the United States for peace were there. I just wanted to go home to bed. I was wiped out, but I went ahead and I did my rap. As I was leaving the church, somebody said, 'The monks are going to lead a march across the Golden Gate Bridge today. Are you going to be there?' I thought, 'Oh my God, I'm wiped out. I've been up all night.' So I said, 'No, I have something I have to do.' Then somebody said, 'Somebody as important as you must be busy.' So I get in my car and start to drive home across the bridge. It is a beautiful sunny day. Then I think, 'Gee, it would be kind of nice to join them.' Those were the ways that I started to get involved. I joined the march just as another marcher and as soon as I get there they ask me to speak. It felt wonderful.

CT: You speak about peace in your public talks?

RD: Yes. My tack is that the only way that peace work works is if the work is done by peaceful people. To be a social activist demands that you work on yourself harder than ever.

CT: There was previously a polarization – you either work on yourself or you work for the planet. But you can work for both.

RD: A lot of people who were political activists in the sixties and anti-spiritual have done a lot of work on themselves since then. All of us realized we were lop-sided. So there is a coming together.

CT: Chogyam Trungpa [late Tibetan meditation teacher] once said at a conference, 'There will be no nuclear war.' I feel such statements give a false feeling of security.

RD: That's interesting. I share Trungpa's feeling that there is not going to be a nuclear holocaust. I mean, a major holocaust. There may be some Three Mile Island errors.

CT: Being European I have a different feeling. Green activists used to say, 'The resources are going to run out.' Now we say, 'Time is running out.'

RD: Fear as a motivator is not a satisfactory way to get rid of the cause of nuclear weapons. I take to task all those who use fear as a motivator for social action. 'We're all in it together,' is the horizontal organization instead of the vertical. For me, Casper Weinberger [one time American Defense Secretary] is me. The world situation is me. As long as we are separate, all motivations for survival as separate entities are going to colour our perceptions. We are not going to be able to deal with the root of the nuclear weapon issue.

CT: I'm not sure there is the awareness of the subtlety of your perception. Rather than seeing the Casper Weinbergers as threats, workshops are taking place where the concept of enemy is seen to be a mind creation.

RD: There is no enemy. It has to do with where you stand in relation to the universe. If you stand anywhere you are a perpetuator of suffering. I'm not interested in symptoms; I'm interested in the root cause.

I live in a slightly different world view than you do. I'm not in the numbers business. Gandhi says, 'Make yourself into zero and your power is invincible.' I'm interested in that domain as much as how many numbers there are in a peace movement. The fabric of world thought is very fragile. A thought can change it just like that. And one event can change all of the thought of the whole system. Shifts in thought have to occur. One of them is by a few people being without fear. There is a purity that can be fed into the system. What Gandhi and Martin Luther King brought into the system was the quality of their being, not just the ability to organize people.

CT: Yourself and others have expressed faith in the unlikelihood of nuclear war. For us in Europe we have the feeling that we just don't know. The security in America over the years has produced a certain optimism.

RD: I have a very close friend. His name is Emmanual and he is not embodied. He is an extraordinary being. I told Emmanual that I work with dying people and asked him what should I tell people about dying. He said, 'Tell them it is absolutely safe, like taking off a tight shoe.' When someone asked about the nuclear threat, he said, 'Don't be silly. School won't be out that soon. How presumptuous to think that they could destroy the world.'

CT: This is an American disembodied spirit!

RD: What Trungpa, Emmanual and I intuitively sense is that the shared awareness of the horror of our predicament has permeated enough into the world that there is less and less likelihood of that happening. Although, it might happen by error or by terrorism.

CT: I think that Trungpa's analogy of two guys, Russia and America, with a knife against each other's throat is a very powerful image. Everybody surely realizes the implications of the situation by now.

RD: I believe that behind the bluff of the poker game there are people who are very much pragmatic, survival-orientated and functional in their way of looking at the universe.

CT: Are you referring to the people in power?

RD: Yes. I realize that I just lost the peace movement with that statement. However, I think these people in power are irrational beings who are caught in power roles in which they must sound and act a certain way but that act does not involve the destruction of the world. I'm certainly not in favour of these people being in power.

In some ways the bomb has already fallen. We are all living with death over our left shoulder; it's never going to go away. We will never undo the knowledge of how to build the bomb even if we get rid of all the tombs. We are just now figuring out what it means to live with death.

CT: Have you been to Europe recently?

RD: No. I do understand that the feelings about the Pershing missiles and all of that are very different there. I live in a relatively protected, isolated country. I don't know whether my feelings about a nuclear war are coming from that conditioning or another place in my being. From my own personal point of view, I do not think it is going to happen. We must listen to the fears of the people who are building the arsenals and help them to devise strategies for feeling safe and independent of nuclear weapons.

CT: As I listened to one of your public talks, I felt you have the capacity to please people which makes the listener very attention to what you have to say. When you mention your views to a broad spectrum of people it may reduce their fears and anxieties about a future nuclear war and so reduces their personal suffering. But, simultaneously, it makes a person feel a bit more comfortable and in that, awareness can fade.

RD: I just said my views into a microphone knowing that those were not popular views. Obviously, I'm willing to say it. That's the first thing. The second is that I told you that I do not work with fear as a motivator for social action. You are asking me not to say something because my saying it will dissipate fear. I agree with you. It will dissipate the fear because I think social action can come out of another place in people. When I was standing with a million people in a demonstration in New York I didn't experience people in fear but a lot of people saying, 'Enough, enough!'

CT: Isn't it just a speculation when you express confidence about the future?

RD: I hear the point. What I notice is that the first reactions people have are fear and urgency, and that impels an action. But, it doesn't have staying power. That's one of the things the peace movement has difficulty with. People won't stay in it because they are coming in and out of those motives and they burn out very fast.

What I am trying to do is to resonate with people from that deeper place within. It is like we are representatives of a higher law in the universe that doesn't allow the thing to go so far off balance that it destroys itself. This is a correcting mechanism that comes from a very deep, intuitive place in people. Your point about knowing the future as a detrimental thing is well taken. Obviously I don't know the future. I live very much in the 'don't know' myself, so how am I going to treat this sense I have that it is not going to happen?

CT: There was a strong belief in England before World War II that it was not going to happen.

RD: Yes. I think you're right. I think that I could make that distinction. I'm trying to support particular actions to prevent what could occur, and yet at the same time, realizing that it might occur. I'm trying to go with that motivation for action. Awareness says, 'I'm part of this whole thing and I must do my part.' I guess when I made those statements they were in reaction to the fears of people. It was to undercut that. That's why I really think that I have been motivated to do that. I think it is not skilful means. I hear what you're saying and I think it is right. Of course, I don't know, but intuitively I don't think it is going to happen. That is my truth. Am I not to share that with you? That's what you are asking me to do. That's what you are saying is skilful means. I say, 'It is never skilful for me not to share my truth.' Do you hear the issue? I have been asked so many times to do something which is deceptive. People have said, 'Look, don't discuss your homosexuality. We don't really want to hear about that.' I say, 'I'm sorry. That is my truth.'

CT: The Buddha made reference to speech. He said: 'Speak that which is both true *and* useful.'

RD: There was a time at the temple when I would become very angry because Maharaj-ji said to me, 'Tell the truth and love people,' but the truth was I didn't love them. Usually what I did was make believe I loved people because that was the acceptable thing to do since I was a devotional yogi. But I decided to tell the truth for a change. And the truth was I didn't love them. So I told everybody I didn't like them and to keep away from me. I was getting more and more furious. One day I threw a plate of food in somebody's face. Maharaj-ji was watching this and he called me over and said, 'Is something troubling you?' I said, 'I hate all of these people. I can't stand myself. My hatred is for everybody. I only love you.' He started to cry and began hitting me on the head. He got milk and poured it down me and said, 'I told you to love everybody.' I said, 'But you told me to tell the truth and the truth is I don't love everybody.' He came up closer and said, 'Love everybody and tell the truth.'

At that moment I saw who I was going to be when I stopped being who I thought I was. I have been dying ever since then into being somebody who loves everybody and tells the truth. You called me on another one, you see. You said, 'The truth *and* what's useful.' OK. I hear it and I hear how I have to work with that.

Recently I wrote down a 'To do' list:

1.   Intend to keep my heart open. Remember what Kabir says, 'Do what you do with another human being but never put them out of your heart.'

2.   Quiet the mind so it is not at the reactive mercy of each passing thought.

3.   Listen with a non-judging, non-craving awareness and to how adversarial positions are reflections of the struggles within myself.

4.   Align my actions with my deepest truth, which is one of harmony.

5.   Help to reframe the context and models in which situations are perceived.

6.   Acknowledge my fear, anger and frustration at the horror and uncertainty of things.

7.   I must reconsecrate myself again and again so that my actions will be as an offering to God by whatever name. To stop complaining and enjoy.

8.   Be responsible but not take organizations too seriously.

9.   Keep my sense of humour.

10.   Accept responsibility in my shared stewardship of the planet, and act. As the Sufis say, 'Trust in Allah but don't forget to tie your camel.'

The issue of acting out of fear and urgency without working on oneself is an interesting one. People don't realize that their greed for 'this' is causing 'that'. If their personal life is all screwed up and they're busy fighting with people, divorcing and all of this kind of stuff, that's as much a contributing factor. We need to listen to the caring language of the heart.

CT: In the peace workshops I ask, 'What's the difference between dying from cancer from radiation fallout and dying from cancer from smoking?'

RD: Exactly. Many people's lives are often a shambles. They are creating waves of anger and unhappiness and they are justifying it all because they're busy with the nuclear issue or some other issue. To me that is very shortsighted and also, it's just not working. Someone like that is a symptom relief person, an allopathic physician, and I'm for going to the root cause.

CT: Women seem to be bringing in a strong intuitive element in looking at the root cause of suffering.

RD: When I was at Harvard in the 1960s, rational thinking was the highly valued strategy in life. Intuition was seen as a weak quality and women were seen as intuitive and, therefore, weak. This was a real put down. I was a part of that because I was part of a junta that demanded more statistics and more experimental methodology. So when I opened through drugs, it was a 180 degree turn for me. It turned out that the intuitive aspect was very harmonious with a part of my being, which is related to my Jewish tradition and my psycho-sexual development.

Women are bringing in new myths as well. When we look at politics in mythic structure there is certainly the need for new myths. As we're moving from the material and analytical levels of reality, if we skip the mythic level and go too fast into the formless level, we miss a very powerful vehicle for social transformation.

CT: Wasn't the myth around a particular figure, the hero, who is going to take the flock to the Promised Land? Well, part of the message of the women's movement is that there will be no individual leaders within the peace movement.

RD: I think that the women's movement has contributed to that but it is not the dominant determinant of it. It's a networking conscious-ness which works at a horizontal rather than a vertical level.

CT: Would you say the lack of the hero is a healthy facet?

RD: It is incredibly healthy. I really think people should be em-powered as individuals. Representative government is second rate compared to government by the people. We are beginning to recog-nize Gandhi's statement: 'Though what you do may seem insignifi-cant, it is very important that you do it.' That's networking. I love it.

CT: Do you see fresh ways in which the peace movement can be explored? What else do you think people can touch their hearts on?

RD: Every ingredient needed to generate the force necessary to change the political reality of the Earth is already present and exists in every individual's heart. What is required to bring that forth is what we talked about earlier, the creation of myths. This allows an individual to acknowledge that part of themselves that previously had been lost in the shuffle – buried underneath economic, psychological, political and social realities.

Bringing in a myth is extremely important. Let's look at Poland. Lech Walesa and some of the people who head Solidarity hold a different myth about what Poland could be, what the power of the individual is and what the government holds. The commitment to their myth was strong enough that the government had to bow down because the myth inflamed the people's hearts; it so touched their hearts.

In the film *Gandhi*, do you remember the non-violent strikers at the salt mine getting beaten up by the army? They were ready to suffer for what they believed without reacting violently. You've got to be ready. That's Christ's message. You've got to be ready for your myth to be strong enough. So, there's the question of who is ready? That is why we have to work on ourselves. That's the essence of Gandhi's message, of Christ's message. In the last analysis we do what we can as part of groups, institutions and movements, but the onus for each of us is to go back in, to work on ourselves, to become that instrument.

As long as there is a flickering place that wants something of the world, including life, you are vulnerable. As long as you are vulnerable, you have a price to pay.

CT: I have been reading the story of Steve Biko, the South African black activist, who was interrogated, tortured and killed by the South African police. Again, the complete commitment, the unwavering commitment.

RD: Most of the people in the social action movement are very idealistic; they're in Wonderland and then you see how they live in their daily life and it's crap. Their marriages, their relations to other people, the drinking, it's not clean. How can they expect to be a soldier of God or be an instrument of that kind of change? That's a big demand on us. The question is whether people are ready to have that asked of them. Nothing less will work. The numbers game is a game of the world. It's not coming out of a feeling of inner strength because people have lost connection with a part of themselves that is strong, that is free. As long as you are not free how can you free anybody? As Gandhi points out, 'When you defeat somebody, you don't win.'

I say, when you go out and get yourself arrested, that's making a statement that is coming out of a very deep place in you. That's a statement to make as an individual; that's wonderful. When you're preoccupied with how many people have sex with you, that is coming out of a different place. In order to make a shift, you've got to get out of the conspiracy or scenario that everybody shares. When I go to India for four months and don't read a newspaper or listen to the news, I'm doing it out of a sense of responsibility, as far as I can see, in order to really hear what's going on within.

Sometimes we look in the wrong place for what is important. I find when I'm teaching there just needs to be one student who hears and I have contributed to a balancing of the whole force in the universe and that will resonate out and out and out. I have found sometimes, too, that when I'm clear enough, I can walk on a stage, just arrange the water pitcher, put my notes down, get the chair ready and by the time I've sat down the whole work is over. It was like mime. It was all a non-verbal communication, just the quality of being, joy, playfulness and lightness and at the same moment, responsibility and patience.

CT: People can be receptive to that.

RD: After I sit down I say, 'Well, that's the lecture, ladies and gentlemen.' That's what we have to demand of ourselves as teachers, Christopher, the integrity of our beings. It's so easy to lose your compassion into the importance of what you think you're doing. There is a strategy of life where you can leave yourself open to that all the time and there is a strategy where you can close to it because it is undermining your ego.

CT: One last question: In the recent past, you have said on different occasions, 'That absolutely blew my mind.' That phrase seems to be a flashback from the late sixties.

RD: I throw in things, like the word 'mentsch', a Yiddish word, then every Jew in the audience says, 'Oh, he's one of us.' 'Blow my mind' is an intentional choice of words. I know that part of the audience is going to feel immediately at home. I use word images to make an intimate communication with a whole variety of people. When I take the same lecture to give to two difference audiences, I examine the metaphors and language I use. I would go to the Hell's Angels to speak and they would all be sitting on their motorcycles and spitting while I am talking. Then immediately afterwards, I go down to Stanford to speak at the university. It sounded like a different lecture but it was exactly the same message. The fun is having no fixed identity.

CT: Thank you, Ram Dass. I enjoyed this time together.

RD: It was fun. There are very few people you actually get a chance to talk to, where you can experience some of the subtleties of how you bring together whatever wisdom you've gleaned into the world, and of how bizarre it often appears.

CT: Let's sit in silence for two or three minutes. Shall we?

Joy without knowing

An interview with Dr Sheila Cassidy
Plymouth, England

In the early 1970s U.S. National Security Advisor Dr Henry Kissinger and the CIA were directly involved in a ruthless campaign to destroy the democratically elected left wing government of Chile, headed by Dr Salvador Allende. Following Dr Allende's death in a military coup in October 1973, the secret police engaged in a nationwide hunt of Allende's supporters. Thousands were hunted down, tortured and murdered.

During those years Dr Sheila Cassidy was working in Chile in an emergency hospital and a shanty town clinic. One day friends asked her to treat a hunted man, who had been shot by the secret police. Dr Cassidy was arrested, tortured and imprisoned for two months. In the face of fear and pain, her religious faith in God and humankind was challenged to the extreme. Amnesty International launched an international outcry against her treatment and that of countless others. She was expelled from Chile in December 1975.

Dr Cassidy spent the next eighteen months campaigning for the release of her fellow prisoners. In 1977 she entered a convent to see whether she had a vocation. 'After eighteen months I was asked to leave because I was ill and unhappy and so in July 1980 I returned to medicine.'

Since 1982 Dr Cassidy has been Medical Director of St Luke's Hospice, Plymouth. In her book *Audacity to Believe* she gives an account of her years in Chile. Her other books include *Prayer for Pilgrims, Sharing the Darkness* and *Good Friday People*. She is also a lecturer, preacher and religious broadcaster.

What immediately struck me upon my arrival at St Luke's Hospice was the cheerful atmosphere, indoors and outdoors. There was a lot of talking and laughter going on. One resident was looking across the bay to dwellings on the further shore. A young mother and child were visiting a young male friend stricken with cancer. I had somewhat expected a silent place, rather like many old people's homes, but here there were children, dogs and laughter.

Dr Cassidy's office seems to be littered with papers, notes and books. 'I am very untidy and disorganised because I'm always trying to cram something else into an overfull life,' she wrote in a one-page biography of herself.

Just before I left she gave me a poem which she had written. One of the verses read:

I believe
no pain is lost,
no fear unmarked.
No cry of anguish
dies unheard,
lost in the hall of gunfire
or blanked out by the padded cell.

I believe that
pain
and prayer
are somehow saved,
processed,
stored,
used in the Divine Economy.

The meeting with her lasted about an hour. We discussed her religious faith. I appreciate immensely her willingness to talk openly and easily about her beliefs and the way her beliefs relate to her perceptions of others, including the dying.

CT: Who are the people that come here to die? What is the relationship of your religious experience to your work with those who are dying?

SC: We look after people who are terminally ill with malignant disease. They come in at any age, from 12 to 100. We often have people who are in their twenties and thirties but most are aged between 50 and 70. They come here primarily for pain and symptom control. For example, if the person has incurable cancer and is experiencing terrible pain, we given them a high priority. We also give high priority to someone who is very frightened. A lot of people come, are treated, and go home again. Others may come and stay here until they die because they are especially vulnerable and needy. We give priority to the young. For example, we had a 26-year-old woman who was here for two months, who died yesterday. She found it very hard to accept that she was dying and fought her illness to the very end, going to a party two days before she died.

CT: How do people find about the hospice?

SC: Mostly they are referred by their general practitioners. St Luke's Hospice is a medical institution, so they come through a medical referral.

CT: I assume that the hospice is not simply for Christians.

SC: The criteria for admission is purely on the physical and emotional needs and our ability to meet those needs.

CT: Are the staff of doctors and nurses expected to have religious beliefs?

SC: The staff must be competent in a clinical way. They must know what they are doing medically and nursing wise. They must have the right type of personality. They have to be down to earth. We have no time for proselytizing Christians who like to shove religion down people's throats. Staff in a hospice must be loving and humour-filled people. This is a place of very basic caring. You have to be able to get your hands dirty and have a sense of humour.

CT: In your book *Sharing the Darkness* you mentioned that you were invited to give a public lecture called 'The Spirituality of Caring'. What does spirituality mean to you?

SC: Spirituality is a rather woolly term. Spirituality deals with our relationship with the unseen God and how we translate that relationship into our relationship with people.

CT: Is a relationship with the unseen God essential for a relationship here with those who are dying?

SC: I think the answer is no. The type of people who work here are nearly always people with some kind of faith. I suspect that people who have faith in an after-life find it easier to spend time day by day with people who are dying. Having said that we have one member of staff who does not believe in God. She is lovely because she believes passionately in people. We like our staff to have a deep faith but we are wary of the person who wishes to convert the world to Jesus.

CT: What does this sense of the unseen God and an after-life provide for you in relationship to those who are dying?

SC: My belief in an unknown and transcendent God is absolutely fundamental to myself as a person and how I live my life. It provides my joy, my everything. My relationship with God is by far the most important thing in my life. It underpins the work that I do.

In terms of my relationship to people I suspect that my belief in God and an after-life makes me very calm in the face of death. Of course, it's much easier to face another's death than one's own. I believe at a deep, gut level that death is not the end but the beginning. I do not mourn for the people I care for although I am sad and distressed when they are distressed and afraid. I believe that when they die they are going on to something new and immeasurably wonderful, so how could I grieve for them, apart from being sad for their families and sometimes missing them myself?

CT: So your belief in an after-life serves as a support for you in your work.

SC: Yes it does, but it also governs my attitude to the people I care for. In a sense what is often difficult for the dying is to be in contact with someone who is embarrassed to talk to them or is unable to talk about death. What we provide that is different from what most doctors and nurses provide is to be very comfortable with the dying.

CT: Are you saying that in a straightforward medical approach the primary consideration is the preservation of the patient's life? You have that consideration too, but you are facilitating a transition as well?

SC: My aim is to assist people to live their lives most fully day by day. I am concerned about the fullness of living rather than the length of days. My conversations with people would not necessarily be overtly spiritual. I would explore what people's beliefs are and what language they use before I got into any God talks.

CT: There is the transition from dying to death which we must face. We cannot say from an experiential standpoint, 'I know what the after-life is.' So this is when faith begins. What is the origin of your faith here?

SC: I think that my faith in an after-life is related to my faith in God in a way that I do not fully understand. I believe I have some kind of experience which is very difficult to pinpoint. It has nothing to do with book learning but only with my inner experience of God.

CT: The inner experience of God gives assurance to faith and to belief in an after-life and something greater?

SC: It is a gamble. At an intellectual level I don't know, but I do believe.

CT: In your book there are many, many quotes from the Bible. The Bible is important to you. The promise in the Bible of moving onto something greater after death is surely only for those who believe in God and, for a Christian, in Jesus too.

SC: I don't believe that. I believe that God IS – whether we believe in Him or not. I don't believe at all that ultimate union with God is dependent upon our faith. I don't believe that Christians have a monopoly on it. I don't think I believe in hell at all.

CT: Isn't what you are saying a heresy?

SC: Is it? Jesus said that in His Father's house there are many mansions. Peter spoke of the net with many different people in it. I am certainly a very liberal Catholic. The conversations I have with my monastic friends do not make me think that I am totally outside the pale!

CT: What are some of the responses to dying that people go through?

SC: I speak a lot about emotional distress in terminal illness; about fear, loss, anger, alienation and despair. The vast majority of people are scared. They experience fear of the unknown, fear of pain and fear of disintegration. I think that is very natural. We have to elicit what people are afraid of and try to help them deal with these fears. But we can only be present for them in their existential fear of the unknown. We can take away a lot of fear but not all of it.

CT: Each person has to cope with the unknown. Are you saying you can go so far with a person but no further?

SC: What I can do is be alongside the person when he or she is frightened. I can give you an analogy. I have to go to the Chilean Embassy. I have to witness with regard to somebody who was murdered in my presence. I have an existential fear of going near Chilean officials because I was imprisoned and done over by them. I have asked somebody from the Foreign Office to come with me. I know that he is not going to protect me but he will accompany me in terms of this foolish fear. I am liberated enough to say: 'I am scared, please come with me.' In the same way we accompany people here with their fears.

CT: Last week my 84-year-old uncle died in a Blackpool hospital. I was with him in his last hours. It was clear to me how much he appreciated my presence as well as the presence of my aunt and my mother.

SC: To be with the dying is a ministry of presence.

CT: Do you think that a belief in God and in an after-life have to go together? Since life is so vast and awesome is it necessary to be concerned with something better later?

SC: The idea of a life after death makes sense to me because there are an awful lot of people who are unable to touch that which I touch and you touch. For example the young woman who died yesterday had a hard life and a hard death. They are cheated people in some ways. It would be naive to imagine that everybody has a deep sense of peace and joy when they die. I was at a meeting this afternoon where we were talking about those who have died here in the last week. This young woman wanted to go on to get married and have children. In a sense it comforts me that there is a beyond. If there is a God of Eternity, who is a just and loving God, then I find it difficult to believe that some people are short-changed for ever. I like to think they will enjoy the fullness of living later. In direct answer to your question I don't think that life after death has to go in with a belief in God but I find it a very useful hypothesis! It works well for me.

CT: You said in your book that your contact with those who experience incredible distress of suffering day in and day out reinforces your faith in a loving God. For some, this faith would seem to be emotionally and intellectually unbridgeable. How is it that your faith is strengthened rather than weakened?

SC: Some of those who experience great pain do also experience great depths of joy; but not all.

CT: What about those who only suffer and know no joy? Their life process has been a hard, painful struggle; the organism has been devastated by the circumstances of life and the person dies painfully right to the bitter end. How can that possibly reinforce faith in a loving God?

SC: I don't know that it does reinforce my faith. What reinforces my faith is when people do experience personal transformation, personal joy. Some years ago I entered a convent wanting to get closer to God. I failed. It didn't work for me. I was very unhappy and I left. Here in an ordinary suburban city I see such goodness from ordinary people. The father of the young woman who died came to the hospice today to pick up his daughter's remaining possessions and the death certificate. He came in his best suit. He was so grateful. I told him that he had been wonderful and so supportive. He said, 'Well, I sat there with my daughter. Sometimes she would be horrible to me, but I knew she didn't mean it so I just took it.' There is such a selflessness in that. Selflessness is one of the holiest things. What reinforces my faith is the selflessness that can be elicited out of very ordinary people. I find that a very holy thing.

CT: It is truly beautiful that people are able to put aside their self-interest for others.

SC: I see so many people who are totally giving. One of the nice things about being here is that you meet people stripped of pretence, in the raw. Some of them are very selfish, but you also see so many people who are so lovely. I find that miraculous. I think the world is bloody marvellous and people are lovely. It is not that I don't know that people are wounded, fragile; but I believe they are fundamentally good.

CT: Your experience in Chile also certainly told you about the range of people's behaviour.

SC: When a dying person feels loved and accepted then the good things in that person begin to come out. We believe that the good is always there in the person even though they may seem initially very selfish.

CT: A loving social environment touches deep places within a person and brings out something profound.

SC: If there is time for it.

CT: A meaningful community endeavours to touch deep places of love, a deep well of goodness within each person. But isn't it possible that this human love is then projected onto a larger dimension called God?

SC: Perhaps the God language provides a language for that which *is*. Christian scriptures provide for me a language for my experience. What I experience which the non-believer doesn't is a personal sense of a relationship with God.

CT: The Christian God is a very personalized form of God. How vital is this God to people, to the dying?

SC: I don't think it is vital at all. One of our staff has no sense of a personal God and she is probably rather more loving and more selfless than I am. I would interpret that as showing that God works in mysterious ways. It's the language, isn't it?

CT: In a way then, the God language isn't so vital.

SC: I have seen people who are equally selfless who are professed believers or professed atheists. I spent a lot of time with Marxists who didn't have a faith. I don't feel any need to convert those who have no faith. In a sense though I do think non-believers are missing out on a certain dimension of joy.

CT: Jesus said that you shall know them by their fruits.

SC: Yes, exactly.

CT: In a way your Christianity is equally a non-Christianity, isn't it?

SC: I am theocentric rather than Christocentric in my worship. I worship the unseen face of God. I quote a lot from the Old Testament. I am equally turned on by the different scriptures. What makes me want to lie on my face in the dark is talk of the unseen transcendent God. I used to say that if somebody discovered that Jesus was not true, I would barely bat an eyelid, but that is not quite as true as it was a while ago. I have been looking a lot lately at the risen Christ and that has become meaningful for me. But what gets me in my religious guts is the sense of the unseen God. That is the God before whom I prostrate.

CT: You come across as closer to the mystical traditions of God rather than to the conventional belief in God the Father and God the Son.

SC: That's true. My belief is deeply rooted in the Christian mystical tradition. I am turned on by the mystics. My experience of God gives me a joy beyond all knowing.

CT: Given your sensibilities and awareness to God, and given the application and the skilfulness of the language which is appropriate to yourself and to those who are dying, do those who are dying change their views very much about life after spending time in a hospice like this?

SC: Some people change a lot. We had a lady recently who came to us frightened, angry and believing she was allergic to the painkillers. She was also resentful of the institution. Over a period of about a month she did a total somersault. She lay there and kept saying to us: 'It sounds crazy but I have never been so happy. I have never known such love exists. I am totally at peace.' She actually came back to her religion, not in a very deep sort of way. She was a lapsed Catholic. She was remarkably at peace. We see that happens for the dying from time to time. It happens enough for us to be very familiar with this kind of change. If people are here long enough it happens often. I think people are amazed at the love they receive. What we offer to people is a non-judgemental relationship. We accept people where they are. If they come with delinquent children and a mistress we don't bat an eyelid. We offer a professional loving which recognises that people are precious whether they are demented or disfigured or behave badly. They are precious quite simply because they are people.

CT: You have the support of God, the support of the social environment and you deal with probably the most difficult period of a person's life, that is their impending death. Amidst all of this is there anything which you regard for yourself as being acutely difficult to acknowledge?

SC: Yes. I don't spend as much time with the patients as I used to. When I began about ten years ago I was the only doctor and I was very close to a lot of people. Now I have a number of different staff. I am heavily engaged in lecturing and I am conscious that I am not as close to them as I used to be.

CT: I can't help noticing the mass of paperwork in your office. Are you bogged down in administration?

SC: It's not so much administration as correspondence about all sorts of things. Sometimes I feel as if I am drowning in paperwork! If I'm rational about my sense of guilt, I would say it is inevitable in my role. I think I run a lovely ship. What I am experiencing is part of the pain of distancing myself because I am at the head of the hospice. The other staff here get both the work and the joy. I am sufficiently close to enough people to know how much I love working with people. Sometimes I have a bit of weariness with the work.

CT: What aspect of the work do you feel some weariness over?

SC: It is a weariness in having close, deep conversations. There is no doubt that one-to-one conversations with dying people are wonderful but draining. Sometimes if I am tired I will step back from it. Quite often I am here until 7 p.m. or 8 p.m. I could be using the time to get close to people. It is not so necessary because others here are doing that. But I don't do it to get on with the paperwork. I am conscious of a degree of distancing.

CT: What gives you renewal when you are weary? You said that you have just written another book. That could be considered an extension of paperwork.

SC: Oh, all sorts of things renew me – television, shopping, especially for clothes, picnics down the river, going for walks, having friends for dinner. The creative side of my nature is very important to me – writing, preparing broadcasts, sewing, playing with my house. I really love the writing – the playing with words and ideas. Prayer and going away on retreat renew me – though in a different sort of way. Retreats can be hard.

CT: In your daily life how much inspiration do you get from the Bible?

SC: What is most important is my relationship with God. The scriptural texts are all part of that. The central thing is to do with the love of God. I suppose that one can experience God in very beautiful surroundings such as when listening to beautiful music or watching a sunset, but you can also experience His presence in very ordinary surroundings. I went to London last week to give a lecture and I sat in an empty tube train going from A to B. I had a tremendous sense of the presence of God, of loving Him and being loved. I felt quite overwhelmed, though at the same time quite aware of where I was.

CT: How much do you value that kind of experience?

SC: I value that kind of experience more than those which come in a more romantic setting. If I experience God when I'm desperate with insomnia or crying or in the tube or car, it seems a more stripped sort of encounter than in the middle of a sunset or a beautiful liturgy. I think that's why I would pray by choice in the dark or in an empty room.

CT: 'Blessed are the poor in spirit for theirs is the Kingdom of God' is the first of the beatitudes of Jesus.

SC: Yes. Words like 'dazzling dark' make me want to lie on the floor and pray. Sometimes I am scared that I kid myself. I don't spend an hour praying every morning. I think if I was really spiritual I would spend an hour every morning and every night praying. In practice maybe I spend half an hour or twenty minutes. It doesn't feel enough but I can't cope with any more at the moment. I can cope with more when I am on holiday. Sometimes I worry about that and sometimes I don't.

CT: Do you pray with words?

SC: No. I don't pray with words. I pray by sitting and opening up myself to God. It is just sitting there. I pray with the odd word. I haven't prayed with words for years and years. I have never been desperately into saying prayers. There is though a certain spiritual pride which comes through praying without words. So I think it is good for me to be able to pray with words also – but the only sort of words I seem to use are 'Help!' or, more often, 'I love You.'

CT: Thank you.

GLOBAL CONCERNS

The pain of the refugee

An interview with Thich Nhat Hanh
Plum Village, Brittany, France

When the United States government sent in hundreds of thousands of troops to wage war on the people of Vietnam, the venerable Thich Nhat Hanh, a Buddhist monk, was leading a contemplative life in the Vietnamese tradition of Buddhism and running a School for Social Services.

Thich Nhat Hanh, known as Thay (teacher), began to speak out about the war and appealed to the North Americans and their allies and the North Vietnamese and the Vietcong to enter into peace negotiations.

He and his students, who were committed to serving the people in the villages, found themselves wedged between the two warring factions. The American military believed they were puppets of the Vietcong and the Vietcong believed they were stooges of the American armed forces. Some of the young men working for the School for Social Services were summarily executed for refusing to take to arms. They experienced food shortages and harassment from those committed to change through violence.

Thay became one of the first major voices in Vietnam to call for the withdrawal of the American forces from his country. That was in 1967. He launched an appeal for a ceasefire while on a visit to Washington. His appeal fell on deaf ears. The war was to escalate even further and to include neighbouring Laos. The widespread bombing of Kampuchea led to a holocaust with the loss of two million lives. Compared to the tragic holocaust of the Second World War the Western world largely turned a blind eye to the immense sorrow of Kampuchea, Laos and Vietnam. None of the North American leaders nor military were brought to trial as war criminals.

It was impossible for Thay to return to Vietnam. Other monks, nuns and laypeople, including co-worker Sister Cao Ngoc Phuong, had to flee Vietnam. In the year before he was assassinated, Martin Luther King nominated Thay for the Nobel Peace Prize. In the years following Thay's arrival in the United States, he and Sister Phuong travelled the world campaigning for peace in Vietnam. He was chairperson of the Buddhist Peace Delegation in Paris during the war.

Since the end of the war in 1975 Thay has continued to travel extensively, giving retreats and workshops for adults and children in the West. He has extensive contact with Vietnamese refugees, both from the war and with the boat people. He has written several books including the best-selling *Being Peace, The Miracle of Mindfulness, Vietnam: The Lotus in the Sea of Fire*, and was co-author with peace activist Daniel Berrigan of *The Raft is Not the Shore*.

Thay is a former vice-chair of the highly respected International Fellowship of Reconciliation and a member of the international advisory board of the Buddhist Peace Fellowship. He is widely loved throughout the international peace movement. One of his poems, 'Please Call Me By My True Names', has been widely reproduced and distributed around the world. Commenting on the poem Thay says: 'I have many names and when you call me by any one of them I have to say "yes".'

This is an extract from the poem.

Do not say that I'll depart tomorrow
because even today I still arrive.

Look deeply: I arrive in every second
to be a bud on a spring branch . . .

I am the mayfly
metamorphosing on the surface of the river.
and I am the bird which, when spring comes,
arrives in time to eat the mayfly . . .

I am the 12-year-old girl, refugee on a small boat
who throws herself into the ocean
after being raped by a sea pirate,
and I am the pirate,
my heart not yet capable of seeing and loving.

My joy is like Spring, so warm it makes flowers bloom.
My pain is like a river of tears,
so full it fills up the four oceans . . .

Please call me by my true names,
so I can wake up,
and so the door of my heart can be left open,
the door of compassion.

I met with Thay in Plum Village, Brittany. For a month in the summer Vietnamese refugees and westerners spend time together.

Meditation, mindfulness practices, informal discussion groups and spiritual teachings make up the daily life for some two hundred men, women and children who go there. Thay loves children. My daughter Nshorna, age 9, who accompanied me to Plum Village, recalls with joy, as I do, her contact with Thay and Sister Phuong. In talking with Thay, I sensed in him a profound goodness and kindness that has not been desecrated by the violence and pain which he and Sister Phuong have witnessed. Both are refugees as well.

The issue of refugees is a major international concern. For example, more refugees from Afghanistan were admitted into Pakistan during the Russian invasion of their country than the number of refugees admitted by the West since the end of the Second World War.

The interview focuses on the pain of being a refugee, cultural adjustments and the application of spiritual practices.

CT: Refugees from Vietnam and Laos come to spend time with you. They are dealing with major upheavals. What do you say to these refugees?

TNH: They have problems that they carry with them and they have problems of living in a strange country. So I address their real problems.

They may have lost someone dear in their homeland or during the trip if they are boat refugees. Their father, mother, son or daughter may have been killed during the trip. They come with a wound within them. Their new country is so different that they have to struggle. Sometimes they cannot integrate but the children can. That will be a problem too. It leaves a gap between themselves and their children – a generation gap and a cultural gap. Refugees often want to retain things that they consider to be precious, beautiful from their culture. Their children don't want these things, may not understand them and are fascinated by the new culture. Parents worry that their children will be dragged into the negative things. Life here in the West is also very busy. They don't have enough time for their children so they are losing real contact with them very quickly, and the children lose their parents very quickly too.

CT: There is suffering of the past through separation, loss and emotional wounds. Parents and children may be in conflict with each other during the transition into a Western society. You must hear this many, many times from refugees you visit in France, Britain, Australia and North America. What do you say to a family wounded, suffering and in conflict?

TNH: I respond by trying to help them understand the causes of their suffering. I propose ways of spiritual practice so they can be relieved of their suffering.

CT: What comes to mind when you think of the causes?

TNH: There are so many causes. They suffer if they keep thinking of the past. I tell them: 'There are many beautiful things in the present moment. You must learn not to cling to what is no longer present. Face life in the present moment.' I teach them how to be in touch with life so they enjoy what is positive in the present moment.

CT: Some parents and grandparents wish to retain something of the old culture. How do you respond to that? There is something to be let go of in the past, the old, yet there is something to be included?

TNH: These things can be described as their cultural heritage. So, when they leave the refugee camps they still have these treasures. They must make good use of these things, like a traveller would, carrying with him or her something on his or her journey abroad. What they think is beautiful and valuable can be applied to their new life. Children can see the beauty of their heritage, receive it and put it into their new life.

CT: As you know, the young become very much impressed with contemporary Western culture. They may regard the older culture as being foreign or distant. Where is the bridge for the young to their cultural heritage?

TNH: I recommend that parents show equal interest in Western society as do the children. I say to the parents, if you don't understand Western culture you will not know how to trust it. I ask, 'What do you consider to be valuable in your own culture?' Your culture should be translated in a form that can be understood and acceptable to your children who are growing in this environment. Culture is the way of living your daily life, the way you walk, the way you eat, the way you treat people, the way you live in your home. There is a Vietnamese way of living and a French way of living. You have got to know about the French way in order to tell your children the best elements in that culture. Refugees have to know the elements not worth adapting to. You compare that with your cultural heritage. You can point out to them what you can learn from the old cultural heritage and what you can learn from the Western culture.

CT: What is useful in our culture? What do you think is questionable and needs to be changed?

TNH: The undesirable elements in a culture bring us suffering. The desirable elements bring happiness, help us grow as individuals, as a family. To get in touch with people you find out what makes them happy, what makes them unhappy and you go to the foundation of that happiness and of that unhappiness. The undesirable element of Western culture is individualism, the belief that happiness is an individual matter. This can be seen very clearly in this culture.

CT: Individualism is a marked feature of Western life.

TNH: The cultural heritage of the West has not been renewed to provide young Western people here with what they really need. More and more flee their own tradition and look for something else. It is like growing plum trees. You should know how to prune the branches that are not necessary, otherwise they will take all of the sap. In a culture it happens that there are branches that take over the place of other branches. When these branches grow too much they destroy the tree itself. People must have the courage of pruning, which is somehow painful. If you can prune you leave space for the tree to bear fruit. That kind of pruning has not been achieved in Western culture so it creates a lot of suffering. For example, the foundation of the family in the West is no longer solid. Christianity is not providing that foundation, that continued support.

CT: By using the metaphor of the tree you demonstrate that there is continual expansionism in Western society without realization of the value of letting go and refinement. Is the expansion of materialism and consumerism what you have in mind?

TNH: Yes. People here want more and more and more. They believe that happiness is the satisfaction of always getting what they want. They don't see that this consumerism destroys their happiness.

CT: How would you describe and speak of happiness as distinct from getting what one wants, from the pursuit of pleasure?

TNH: The sole pursuit of pleasure brings about displeasure later. If we have a deep understanding of pleasant feelings we know that it is not really pleasure that nourishes us. There are other pleasant feelings that can never harm us, that do nourish us and help us to grow.

CT: What are these pleasant feelings that emerge and that are the result of self interest? What are the pleasant feelings that nourish us and enable us to grow?

TNH: When you sit here you feel the breeze. You are with nature, with the healthy elements of life. That kind of pleasure is not destructive. But when you consume alcohol you know that although it is a pleasant feeling it is destroying your body and your nervous system. If we only think of pleasure without seeing the nature of the pleasure then we will suffer.

CT: This requires the ability to discern happiness and the pleasure, to understand what contributes to growth and what contributes to our harm.

TNH: We should not be afraid of our natural pleasurable things. Let us realise that these pleasant feelings can only help us grow, make us happy. When we are happy we make other people happy.

CT: Could I relate that to the issue of refugees? Refugees wish to retain their culture, their beautiful traditional values which give happiness but which don't bring harm. In the West there is often a lot of public debate suggesting that people from traditional societies who have come to live in the West have become too isolated from the mainstream of society here – Muslims, Hindus, Sikhs, Buddhists and various ethnic groups.

TNH: Beauty has universal values. If you know that you will make your values acceptable to other groups. The old culture may need some transformation in order for it to become accepted in the new culture. It is like traditions of cooking that belong to a culture. A dish in India imported to France should be transformed a little bit in order to fit the French taste. There are Indians who live or are born in France who prefer another version of the dish. I think if the elements of an ancient culture remain exactly the same in a foreign land it would have less opportunity to be accepted by others.

CT: Does this apply to the Buddha's teachings?

TNH: We need new forms of language to give the message of the Buddha on the Four Noble Truths.

CT: It is sometimes thought that Buddhism is somewhat disengaged from life, from various social concerns. I was a Buddhist monk in Thailand and India from 1970 to 1976. It certainly appeared that way at times.

TNH: In some forms of spiritual practice Buddhism will look like withdrawal from life. To me Buddhism should be engaged in order to be called Buddhism. The teaching is to solve problems, not to take you away from life. Therefore teachers have to address real problems of society and of individuals and propose practical ways for people to see into the nature of undesirable situations. To me, if Buddhism is not engaged in social issues it is not real Buddhism. A religion which is not useful will vanish. Buddhism needs renewal. In the history of 2,600 years of Buddhism there have been many attempts to renew Buddhism. I see that Buddhism here should be different. Buddhism should be distinguished from culture. Buddhism is very often mixed up with a local culture.

CT: Don't your robes indicate a culture?

TNH: Yes. To me Buddhism should be made of elements of the local culture. To build a house it is better to take your materials from the local forest. Essentially building the house is the same everywhere. I have been encouraging Buddhists in the West to make good use of elements within Christianity and Judaism. I don't mind at all if people chant the Heart Sutra with a Jewish liturgy. It is easier to move the hearts of people with local elements of their culture.

CT: But many people do not feel any association with orthodox Western religion. Many adults here have no history of religion or church going. Some people in the West claim they have no relationship at all to any religious tradition.

TNH: The seeds of tradition are in the blood of people. People cannot be without culture and a tradition, although they may hate it. Sometimes they say, I don't want to have anything to do with my father. But they are a continuation of their father. Thinking is one thing and reality is another. We should encourage them to turn to their culture because their roots are there. They are not really uprooted. Westerners are still rooted in their culture. They can discover the values in their tradition. Buddhism can be a kind of stimulus to help them to feel rooted again. So, my voice is not telling you to leave your culture. I say the opposite: go to your culture and be happy. That is my approach.

CT: In Western religious culture, the word 'God' is a central element in the religious fabric. In Buddhism we do not use the word 'God'. Buddhism could be thought of as atheistic. How do you view that in terms of bridging the gap between different religious cultures?

TNH: I think it is better to present Buddhism not as a religion. I think it is important to present the Buddha as a teacher. In Christianity, there are theologians who can think of God not as a person but as the ground of being. Ground of being is something like the Dharmakaya in Buddhism. More theologians today have contact with Asian religions where they seek a language to express elements that have been neglected in Christianity and Judaism. We serve as stimuli in order to help them to bring these things out. We also say that the 'mind' is the artist that draws the world, draws happiness and draws suffering. If we are in touch with the deepest level of our mind, we will discover a source of joy, of understanding, of happiness – so Mind is God.

When I speak of non-duality I say that the rose and the rubbish 'inter-are'. This is the very heart of Buddhism. The organic gardener takes care of the garbage. He is not running away from the rubbish because he knows that the garbage will bring the flower back. So there is no gap between the ultimate and the practical.

CT: Dharma teachings embrace the duality of the rose and the garbage. Your teachings explore ways to understand and embrace both the garbage and the rose.

TNH: Yes. In us there is a rose and there is garbage. We should not be afraid of the garbage in us. The moment we accept that, we have peace. We are peaceful because we know how to accept and use these experiences. We know that we can learn ways to transform them so the rose goes into garbage, and the garbage goes back to rose. We are not afraid, we know the techniques, so we can live peacefully without fear.

CT: In the teachings you encourage people to smile. Some listeners don't quite understand this. Why is smiling important to you?

TNH: When there is a pleasant feeling, you know there is a pleasant feeling.

CT: But you are smiling to introduce the pleasant feeling – not just feel it when it arises.

TNH: In the Discourse of Mindfulness of Breathing, the Buddha said 'to feel happy'. Smiling is only an expression of that, to make it concrete.

CT: A person might say, 'But if I'm feeling sad and I smile, I am not being true to my feelings.'

TNH: Smiling alters the body – particularly your mouth. Something happening in the spirit can be translated into the body. But we don't allow that. What is happening in the body will have an effect. Practice mouth yoga, smile like that, and suddenly you have a pleasant feeling. Mouth yoga is what happens in the realm of the body and then a pleasant feeling will be born in the realm of the spirit.

CT: You are saying that by introducing a pleasant feeling into the body it naturally communicates into one's heart.

TNH: Yes. There is a change in your spirit. The body has the right to initiate these changes. Then you can even smile to your suffering. If you smile to your suffering you increase your strength. You are being compassionate to yourself.

CT: The power of the pleasant feeling in the smile is to transform the spirit, the inner life. Isn't there the danger that in smiling we may lose the critical faculty?

TNH: In Western psychotherapy and Western medicine, you pay attention to what is wrong. If you use all your time paying attention to what is wrong you lose the opportunity to get in touch with what is *not* wrong. You have to practise joy also. So we practise to be aware of suffering in order to transform it. We also practise to be in touch with the joy in order to become strong. You take vitamins with the medicine. This is only to re-establish the balance. If a bamboo is too dry on one side and you want to correct it, you will overbend it a little bit so it will become straight.

CT: You are saying that Westerners are too much involved in suffering, too much concerned with what is wrong.

TNH: Yes. Too much suffering kills the spirit, makes your heart become a stone. Everything requires balance.

CT: Do you think there is a danger of becoming saintly, so that we neglect an analysis of major social, political, economic and environmental issues? Where is the relationship between being warm and caring, and looking into the global problems which are serious for our planet?

TNH: Personal problems are connected to the social, global problems. Psychotherapists know that society is creating more clients for them but they have to make time to heal society, so it does not create so many sick, unhappy and confused people.

CT: Doctors and psychotherapists make people well only to send them back into the society which made them sick to begin with.

TNH: Yes. We have to begin at home. In the family, you have to look into the problems of your son, daughter, husband, wife. Through these people you see society. Dealing with the family means to deal with members of society. If you practise mindfulness and awareness, you ask your children to be careful about the garbage. When you throw banana peels into the compost heap you experience a pleasant feeling. You know that the banana peel can be recycled as a lettuce. If you throw away a plastic bag with mindfulness you know that it is different. The feeling is uneasy. The plastic bag will take much more time to go back to being a lettuce. When you throw away plastic diapers, they take 400 years to dissolve into the earth. If you are aware that nuclear waste is a kind of garbage then you feel very, very concerned because it takes 250,000 years to recycle. Considering garbage is to be involved in social action. That affects your children and their children. Generations of families will be affected by the way we use our garbage.

CT: There is a small but growing active public awareness of these problems. Can you differ between spiritual awareness and mindfulness, and conservation awareness?

TNH: Mindfulness is the moment you begin to see clearly. The insights have an impact on our behaviour in the domain of family life and social life. We find out ways to awaken people. I think that Buddhism in the West should ally itself with groups like ecologists, feminists, psychotherapists, peace activists. We can learn from them and they can benefit from our practice of awareness. An ecologist is someone aware of what is going on in the realm of ecology. So she is practising Buddhism, she is a friend of mine, she can teach me many things. I can support her in the practice of mindfulness and bring the techniques of Buddhism to her. We can have such a relationship with psychotherapists, peace activists, feminists. They are all future Buddhas.

CT: It is understandable if other societies blame the West for its long history of colonialism and consumerism. What can enable people to understand Western culture without being angry and resentful? More and more people in the rest of the world point a finger to the West as having to take a lot of responsibility for global realities.

TNH: People in the West accuse themselves as well. We must demonstrate that a simple lifestyle can be very happy. That is about the only thing we can do to help. When the West tries that kind of life they can get rid of their worries and their depressions. The West needs to *believe* we can be happy consuming much less.

CT: Yet many people throughout the world wish to imitate the West, to take the path of consumerism. They say it is easier for us to let go of consumerism because we have had it. They say, 'But we haven't had it, we have to go through this stage.'

TNH: We accept each other much more easily if we understand each other's suffering. This is the core of the Buddhist practice; leading a simple life is only one aspect. Look deeply in order to understand the other person. When you understand you are moved by their suffering. We must try to listen to each other, including children, in order to understand the problems and suffering of each other. That is very helpful. Then we bring out our own experience in dealing with suffering. We exchange experience. We shine the light of dharma on suffering. We transform our being together into a kind of workshop, where we can crystallise a number of methods so that we may share what we learn with other communities.

CT: Thank you, Thay.

Dealing with the death squads

An interview with Joe Gorin
Barre, Massachusetts, USA

Joe Gorin is fond of calling himself 'Buwish'. In the last twenty years a number of Jews travelled extensively, particularly to India and the Far East, to explore other religious traditions. It was not a case of dismissing their religion of birth, namely Judaism, but rather exploring the depths of the spiritual life. Such people came to be referred to in a light-hearted way as 'Buwish' – a combination of Buddhist and Jewish.

Joe Gorin took part in his first intensive insight meditation retreat in Barre, in the western part of Massachusetts, in 1978. He was born into a Jewish family in Cambridge, near Boston, in the United States. He took a degree in psychology and became a psychotherapist working in a clinic and in private practice.

During the years of spiritual practice he came to realize the significance of the relationship between unresolved emotional and psychological forces and the way that they influence political actions. He perceived that there were people in this world with immense political influence who were basically living out their unresolved problems around violence and fear.

He became a member of the national board of the Buddhist Peace Fellowship in the United States, and participated in meetings to discuss non-violence both as an ethical foundation for spiritual life and as a strategy. Joe also participated in a number of campaigns to halt Washington's support of right-wing regimes in Central America.

I remember participating in a small group meeting of peace activists in a private house in Leverett, Mass., with Joe, two prominent political activists and organisers, Paula Green and Jim Perkins (see the interview in *Spirit for Change*), Dave Dellinger, who was one of the Chicago Seven put on trial twenty years ago, and other activists involved in the Witness for Peace campaign. We saw a film of a Contra attack on a lorry in Nicaragua, and a reminder of the suffering that firearms inflict on their victims.

Some of the activists, including Joe, had travelled to the borders of Nicaragua and Honduras to witness for peace. The witnesses would stand in the hills of the trouble spots, live in the villages and thus inhibit the Contras from launching attacks on the people who lived in the region.

It was well known that if US citizens were harmed in the war funded by their government and right-wing businesses, the American public would demand a total end to support for the Contra. It was a high-risk strategy but it saved lives and the witnesses could report back to the international media what they saw.

In 1987 Joe decided to quit his job as a psychotherapist and work in Guatemala to give personal support to those threatened by the death squads. He also spent time in Nicaragua and El Salvador.

In August 1989 he returned to the United States from Central America. Two days after his return he came to participate in a retreat with me at the Insight Meditation Society in Barre. It was at this time that I recorded the interview.

Following his return, Joe has worked on a book of his experiences, *Choose Love: A Jewish-Buddhist Human Rights Worker in Central America*. He has spoken at numerous meetings about the situation in Central America. 'The nine-year-old girl I saw in the remote village of Cuatro Equinas in Nicaragua was killed by bullets that were paid for with our tax dollars.'

At the present time Joe is living in the working class neighbourhood of Mt. Pleasant in the District of Columbia, and is the director of the Network in Solidarity with the People of Guatemala (NSGUA). He told me when he goes to the local stores he converses with the shopkeepers in Spanish.

CT: Nine days ago you returned from Central America. Before you went you were working as a psychotherapist. What was your intention in going to Central America?

JG: I went there in July 1987. I had been working as a psychologist for ten or eleven years, doing a great deal of psychotherapy, training students and consultation with community agencies. I started coming to the Insight Meditation Society in about 1978, about the same time I started doing psychotherapy. During all this time I was politically active since the Vietnam War. Insight Meditation informed my activism to a great degree. In 1984 Erik Kolvig, Paula Green and myself formed the Western Massachusetts Chapter of the Buddhist Peace Fellowship. I later joined the Board of Directors of that organisation. We organized a trip to Nicaragua with the Fellowship of Reconciliation. I had become increasingly active in Central American issues in the early 1980s when a close friend of mine had been abducted, tortured and killed by a death squad in Guatemala in 1980. That altered my interest a great deal. He had moved down there in 1976 and had been there for four years at the time of his abduction and assassination. I started to relearn Spanish. I had been around it a lot as a kid, so it came back to me fairly easily. I became involved in issues around Nicaragua and El Salvador. An El Salvadorian refugee who had to flee that country lives at my house because I was the only person in the neighbourhood who spoke Spanish. I also became involved with the local Quakers who were giving sanctuary to a couple of Guatemalan refugees. My passion was the struggle in Central America. It became clear to me that my full aliveness was not happening in my work as a psychologist but in issues of Central America. So I have lived there for the past two years when I led this delegation of Buddhist Peace Fellowship and the Fellowship of Reconciliation people to Honduras and Nicaragua. Then I started working for Peace Brigades International, an international group based on Gandhi's concept of non-violence, born out of the conflict between India and Pakistan. Civilians would interpose their bodies between conflicting armies. Today Peace Brigades in Guatemala works with people threatened by death squads and paramilitary death squads and other potential victims of political violence.

CT: These people in the Peace Brigades: were they Guatemalans or from overseas?

JG: There were no Guatemalans. It was considered unsafe for Guatemalans to join this particular group. Guatemala is concerned about its overseas image, particularly in Europe and North America. The death squads involved in disappearances and assassinations are somewhat loth to involve North Americans and Europeans for fear of tarnishing their image in those places.

CT: What kind of numbers have disappeared in Guatemala?

JG: In 1954 there was a popularly elected government which the CIA lead a coup against. In the last twenty years there have been 100,000 political extra-judicial assassinations and 40,000 disappearances. There are about one million exiles and internally displaced people. This means that the people were forced to move to some other part of the country, or escape into the mountains to flee the army.

CT: Does Peace Brigades have an office in the capital or is it a secret organisation?

JG: The headquarters is in the capital city. They also have established a centre in Quiche Province. When I started with Peace

Brigades we only had one person who would go up to the Quiche, probably the most dangerous area. I was that particular person. I spent a moderate amount of time outside the capital, working specifically with a couple of people. One man, Amilcar Mendez, is frequently threatened because he is leading a group trying to dissolve the Civil Patrols, which are these legalised paramilitary groups. The government has created these compulsory Civil Patrols of civilian males, between the ages of 15 and 50. It is a key part of the counter insurgency. The Guatemalan constitution states that these are voluntary. In fact, they have about 800,000 men involved and virtually all of them have been threatened or intimidated into joining. So, I did a lot of work with Amilcar by accompanying him when he had to go on dangerous missions.

CT: Did Peace Brigades International give you any advice, training or instruction?

JG: Yes, we had a training period. We had a lot of reading to do beforehand and we had weekly team meetings to discuss the situation. There were people from the Grupo de Apoyo Mutuo ('Relatives of the Disappeared' – literally translated: Group for Mutual Support). We would frequently accompany members of that group, one of whom was six years old. She is the daughter of the president of this group. This little girl received frequent death threats. We had to accompany her almost twenty four hours a day. Her father had been disappeared by security forces when she was an infant. She was targetted because of her mother's political activity. We also had much contact with workers. At one particular plant occupation we had a twenty four hour presence.

CT: You speak of accompanying somebody around the clock. What does that mean?

JG: Sometimes, we would accompany them from their house to their place of work. For example, we would accompany a teacher to their school, stand outside the school for 3, 4, 5 hours then accompany them back home. Somebody might want to meet a co-worker down town. We would look around to see who was in the restaurant. Did anyone look fishy? We would want to know where the exits are.

CT: Did you put out that you were North American and not a Central American?

JG: There is quite a noticeable racial difference. The Guatemalans are considerably darker, so there would be little likelihood of that confusion. But, it was known that a lot of the people we accompanied were highly visible. They were in the newspapers all the time. The death squads, the government and the military all knew these people were being accompanied by internationals, either European or North American.

CT: How do they feel having you like a shadow with them all the time?

JG: Usually there was a very warm and loving relationship. But there was one particular person I used to accompany who resented her escorts. I started having thoughts like, 'This ingrate doesn't deserve me,' so I could see quite readily that all my motivations were not coming out of humanitarian and political dedication. Part of me was doing this because I wanted to be loved and appreciated. That gave me cause for considerable self reflection. Of course, I came to understand why someone might feel aversion to being constantly shadowed by someone.

CT: Were there situations where there was a real threat?

JG: During the first eight or nine months in Guatemala I worked with Peace Brigades, then in the Nicaraguan War Zone and then for another period in Guatemala. During this first period I was the chauffeur for a group of four exiles who came back, one of whom was Rigoberta Menchu. There is a movie about her called 'When the Mountains Tremble'. These four very highly visible political exiles were front page news in Guatemala for weeks before they came home. Their whole arrival was one of the most controversial things that happened in Guatemala. There were lots of threats against them. Security was very tight, Rigoberta was arrested on arriving but immediately released due to international pressure. I was chauffeuring them around and they also had a police escort, so I had to make sure that the police were following me. It is not very reassuring to know that some of the police who are the authors of these tragedies are your protectors. On another occasion a student activist was murdered. Her sister, who looked almost exactly like her, was frightened she might be a target. She was trying to get out of the country fast. I was accompanying her during her last days in Guatemala with the probability of death squads looking for her. At one safe house we heard what sounded like someone trying to break in. On numerous times I was approached on the street by strangers asking me who I was, or what I was doing. It was hard to tell whether I was being paranoid or not.

CT: What is the channel for threatened people to get out of the country?

JG: The common way is what they call 'mojado' (wet) – just going illegally, through Mexico and into the US. Canada has a programme to take in people who are threatened by political violence. One must be able to prove it. The murdered woman, whose name was Elizabeth, had gone to the Canadian embassy about a year before saying, 'The death squads are following me. Can you get me out of the country?' She could not prove it, so they did not get her out. Amnesty International also intervenes. I was working with a woman recently whom Americans Watch helped to get a temporary tourist visa to the US. Sixteen members of her family have disappeared or have been murdered. The death squads were combing everywhere for her to make her number 17. However, her US visa is only good for a year.

CT: How did you take care of your food, money, health and accommodation?

JG: I had room, board and $50 a month from Peace Brigades. I also received donations from international friends who believed in what I was doing and wanted to support me.

On one occasion I had gone to El Salvador. Peace Brigades has a team there; I had gone to translate at an international meeting. My first day there I went by the US Embassy. It is a fortress. There is a fence with electrified barbed wire on top, and a sheer mass of concrete wall. On the wall there is all this wonderful high-quality graffiti.

CT: What did it say?

JG: One said in Spanish, 'Aqui se planifican los masacres del pueblo Salvadoreno' (This is where the massacres of the Salvadorian people are planned). It says this in big letters on the wall of the US Embassy. I knew that it is a 'No, No' taking pictures of embassies and military but I could not resist. The coast looked clear, I pulled out my camera, took a photograph, put the camera back in my backpack and was feeling very smug. When all of a sudden I found myself surrounded by Salvadorian police. If my mission here was found out by the Salvadorian police it could compromise the security of Peace Brigades. I acted like dumb tourist, which came distressingly easily! 'Oh gee, I'm sorry.' They took my passport, I travel with non-political books, I had Jack Kerouac's *On the Road*. I'm alternately reading this and wondering about life in a Salvadorian prison. They had gone over to the embassy. Two guys appeared, clearly C.I.A., sunglasses, casually dressed, and suggested I enter the embassy with them to be interviewed by the US Consul General. I have a number of friends who had gone with the Salvadorian police, so I said, 'Sure, I'll talk to the Consul General.' I continued to behave like a dumb tourist. 'How long do you plan to be in El Salvador?' 'Two weeks.' What was my work? I said, 'Psychologist.' I began to bore him to tears with details about my career. He invited me to a wine and cheese party they were having right there. I said, 'No thanks!'

CT: What were your feelings towards him?

JG: I spoke to the Consul General for about half an hour, during which time I came to like him. He became more of a human being than a Consul General. This brought up for me a dilemma that I had to wrestle with many times during my two years in Central America: how do I reconcile the fact that this is a fellow human being, with frailties, fears and loves, who I find likeable and engaging, with the fact that he is a mildly important cog in one of the world's most oppressive security operations?

People in El Salvador are very much at risk. There are a lot of arrests and detentions. We received a communication from a group of Guatemalan exiles who had found out about aerial bombardments of the civilian population in the northern part of Quiche. So I was selected to go up to the northern part of Quiche in the Ixil Triangle. It is a conflict zone. I went up to the military base and knocked on the door and said, "Hi, is the Commandant home?" I met him and we spoke about aerial bombardments. According to our reports, and to eye witnesses whom I spoke with, the army was bombing civilian populations. The civilian population of the area had fled to the mountains to escape the arbitrary massacres. The army wanted these people back down from the mountains because they wanted to have them under their control. These people were reputed to be the social base of the guerrillas. Guatemala has the longest standing continuous guerrilla insurgency – about 28 years – in the hemisphere if not the world. The army would go up with helicopters and, using people's full names, would say, 'Come back to Nebaj [the principle town]. If you don't come back we are going to bomb this area.' The Commandant was this charming, funny, intelligent guy who, like the Consul General, I couldn't help but like, although I knew this man was murdering civilians. My goal wasn't to get him to stop bombing. It was to advise him that the international community was aware of what was happening. They have to then take this into account.

CT: What was the response from the Commandant?

JG: The moment I sat down in his office, he went right for the jugular. He said, 'What is the legal status of your group in our country?' We don't have legal status. So, I deftly handled that one. Our application actually got up to the President of the Republic's office. The President did not want to be the one to reject it, so he sent it back down and asked them to reject it, but it hadn't been rejected yet. I said, 'The only thing we are waiting for is the President's signature.' One develops a different sense of right speech in such situations!

CT: Did you ask him directly about the bombing?

JG: I asked about the bombing. He said, 'It's not true. Don't believe it. Don't believe everything you read.' Then he said 'Do you know who Rigoberta Menchu us?' I said, 'The name sounds familiar.' She is a friend who is one of the most powerful and articulate voices of opposition in Guatemala. He said 'Menchu! She says we are trying to commit genocide. 60% of the population is indigenous, so if we were to commit genocide, we would have to kill just about everyone. Genocide is completely impractical!' Being Jewish I get nervous when I hear talk about genocide being impractical. There is a quiet genocide going on in Guatemala, 100,000 murdered, the vast majority of whom are indigenous.

There were times when I wanted to kill him and I suppose he wanted to kill me. Yet at other times, he was very human. The fact that he was not a personification of a Hollywood villain made it harder to deal with.

CT: During your time in Central America you sent out a considerable number of letters.

JG: I was sending out about one letter a month. These were pretty thick letters, they were about eight single-space typewritten pages about my perceptions, my experiences. They were cathartic for me and also let people know what was happening. It was also a form of my giving back something to the literally hundreds of people who had supported me during this time.

CT: So, from Guatemala you went into Nicaragua. Once again to meet with the Peace Brigades?

JG: In Nicaragua I was working with Witness for Peace, which is a different group. It is a Christian group. I am a Jewish Buddhist. People were interested to see what a Jewish Buddhist looked like. I began to develop a great appreciation for the model of Christian based communities. The communities gather together to reflect on the teachings of the Bible and act on those reflections.

CT: Is it born out of the insights of the liberation theology movement?

JG: Yes. One of my sources of optimism for Central America and Latin America is the reawakening of the church which is happening through liberation theology. I actually was able to make sense out of the Bible for the first time. I developed a great appreciation for the life and teachings of Jesus. My mother would get very nervous if she knew this. Hard-line Marxists say, owning class and working class are in inherent conflict; they can never work it out. Christian democrats say there is no inherent conflict; they just have to communicate better. Liberation theologians give a different perspective. They say it is in the interest of the wealthy to stop oppressing and using people. People can't be free until the oppressed person is free.

CT: Liberation is not separate from interconnectedness.

JG: The freedom of us all is in fact interconnected. No one of us is free until all of us are free. Dharma teachings influenced me in a very real way. Working with Central Americans I came to see my liberation is tied up with the freedom of Central Americans and with all oppressed people. I wasn't working so that Guatemalans could be free, but so that we could all be free, all be liberated. I was often exploring interconnectedness and how my fate and their fate were one. I have never been in the mainstream of society but I have never felt oppressed. There I had to work very discreetly, I got the sense of what it is to be oppressed. I saw the way the wheel turns: now I am part of a privileged elite, now the wheel turns and I am part of an oppressed group. I came to identify the part of me that has always been oppressed and that has always had some natural resonance with those who are oppressed by systems.

CT: How do actions reveal interconnectedness?

JG: For example by boycotting Coca-Cola, we feel a connection with people in South Africa, it could end up someday being the privileged elite. I think this is what Jesus meant when said that a rich person can't enter the Kingdom of Heaven any easier than a camel can pass through the eye of a needle. I think what he was saying was that as long as one person is benefitting from the suffering of others then the Kingdom of Heaven is not available. We all profit from it if we live in the US, Europe, South Africa or Australia.

CT: In Nicaragua, these communities exist alongside a continuing threat from the Contra. What was your relationship to both?

JG: I lived in the war zone, known as Region 5. It is the part looking towards Costa Rica, not far from Bluefields. The Contra are quite active there. I would see a US paper and I would hear the war was over. Unfortunately the Contra hadn't read those same newspapers! There was a lot of Contra activity, kidnappings, attacks on villages, thefts on the roads. I had three basic functions: to document human rights abuses, taking delegations around the war zone to meet people, and 'Standing with the People'. You once pointed out that we are human beings not human doings. We were being with the people, living the lives they were living. We had a very good network of information about how the war was affecting the civilian population. About 40-45,000 people would receive our information in the US.

CT: How do you document human rights abuses? How fearful are the people of actually communicating what is happening?

JG: I didn't see that much fear from the people in Nicaragua. I saw a great deal in Guatemala. One has to earn the confidence of people who are loth to speak. In Nicaragua people take automatically to Gringos because most North Americans in Nicaragua were supporting the people in the war zone and working against the policy of the US government. People in the area thought that everyone in the US were dedicated, peace loving people and that Ronald Reagan had nothing to do with the people of the US. They wanted people in the US to know what happened in their little tiny villages. When there was an attack we would talk to witnesses, to survivors.

I remember once in the town of Jacinto Baca, we had to take an hour-and-a-half bus ride and then walk four hours. Between where the bus stops and Jacinto Baca the Contra had done about five kidnappings in the week preceding and had mined the road. We had been sent to find out the details because there had been several witnesses. In the war zone there is always rifle fire. Usually a soldier firing into the bushes to make sure it is not somebody who is going to shoot him. My co-worker said to me, 'Gee, I hope we don't get kidnapped. Tomorrow, it's my birthday.' Later in the month I was writing my monthly letter and I realized that that was a fairly peculiar thing to say. At the time it did not seem peculiar at all. What would we say to the Contra if we were kidnapped? It was a relevant question because Witness for Peace people had been kidnapped three times by the Contra.

CT: Do you ever question how effective your work is?

JG: In the US, we tend to judge effectiveness in terms of short-term results. For example, many activists became burned out when it took years of work to bring the Vietnam war to an end. Many bought into the myth perpetuated by the media and the power elite that the end of that war had nothing to do with internal dissent. Subsequent revelations indicate that both Republicans and Democrats feared that if the war were not ended, there could be massive social upheaval in the streets of the United States that could threaten their hold on power. But if we look for short-term results that are defined by external changes, we are doomed to feel ineffective. If I need Ronald Reagan to change in order for me to feel effective, I have created a structure designed to guarantee ineffectiveness.

But when we take the long view, we can see that the tide of history is rolling towards liberation. Since the nineteenth century, we have ended slavery, achieved women's suffrage and instituted child labour laws. The women's movement has made giant strides in asserting the full dignity of women, racial discrimination in the States is illegal and the US can no longer overtly support puppet military dictators or involve itself in prolonged troop invasions. To feel ineffective, we have to deny history. Of course many activists break out in hives when they hear these things. They would respond that sexism, racism, militarism and exploitation are still rampant. While this response is accurate, it denies the historical process of which we are part.

CT: How do you deal with fear?

JG: I and other co-workers truly realized that fear is just a conditioned response. When I was surrounded by constant potential danger I began to develop a different response. I remember having heard people say that fear is our friend because it lets us know when we are in danger. I don't buy that, I don't buy it in my own experience. When there is danger one can respond with the simple recognition of danger. That is different from fear. I would recognise danger and take whatever precaution was necessary. For example, just a few days before I left, I was involved in a potentially dangerous situation, while trying to help get my friend Fladio Panteleon out of the country. He worked with the Coca-Cola Union in their theatre group. This theatre group for campesinos [peasants] lampooned the army. One night, after a performance, he was surrounded by men who shot him in the foot. After that point he and his brother had to leave their home. His brother Rolando, a friend of mine, was later abducted, tortured and assassinated. Death squads were looking all over for Fladio. Canada and Amnesty International interceded. He was going to get out. We then found out that the death squads were asking nearby for him. We had to get the family out of the area. At this point Fladio, his wife and two little boys, aged three and one, moved in with me. It very often happens that somebody just about to leave gets assassinated.

We found another house. I borrowed a vehicle from a delegation I was working with and I asked four of them to volunteer for this mission. The mission was to get his family into the van, hidden and driven to the safe house. We knew the street was being watched. Everyone from the delegation volunteered but there is only so much space in the vehicle. We put on our sunglasses and cameras so as to look and behave like tourists. We picked the family up, whisked them into the van, drove past the new safe house several times to make sure it was not being watched. Fladio and the family are now in Canada, along with two other people from the theatre group. What was most interesting about this was that everyone in the van was fully aware of the danger of what we were doing and yet no one was afraid.

CT: Did your years of experience in insight meditation and as a psychotherapist play a part in your own relationship to your activities in Central America?

JG: The insights which have come to me through meditation are the very foundation of the way I am in the world. The difference between what is often called 'spiritual practice' and the actuality of who I am and what I do has become increasingly merged. My activities in Central America were every bit as much a part of my spiritual practice as sitting meditating. The Buddha and other great teachers have pointed to the importance of the development of compassion. It seems to me that compassion without action is pity and pity is a characteristic that rigidifies the boundary between self and other. This is not what the Buddha was talking about.

CT: How would you describe your spiritual practice in Central America?

JG: In a conscious way, my work of these past two years has been a loving kindness meditation. But my actual 'spiritual' path took particular forms over this period. I found it very difficult to do formal sitting meditation in a war zone, although I'm sure it could be done. It is hard to just note 'hearing, hearing' when what I was hearing was an AK-47 submachine gun being fired a few hundred yards away. But when I would meet people like the US Consul General in El Salvador or the commandants of El Quiche, my first general reaction was to try to wish them out of existence, because I felt that their 'jobs' involved the institutionalization of the three mental poisons of greed, aggression and delusion and that they were responsible for widespread suffering. But I would not accept this reaction on my part as being any more or less solid than 'hearing, hearing'. I would try to see the Buddha within them, although I often failed. I would often reflect on how one can participate in a liberation movement without creating an us-and-them. I accepted this question as a sort of Zen koan.

I want to encourage people to act. Look at what the next step is. It might be to write a letter to a Congressman, to work with others, demonstrating on the streets, resisting taxes, going to jail, or going to visit these areas of conflict. I always viewed my work in Central America as a support for people serving others here.

The word 'protest'; the etymology is 'pro' meaning for or in favour of, and 'test' meaning testify. Protest means *to witness in favour of*. Another word is 'conspiracy'; 'con' means with, and 'spire' meaning to breathe (as in inspire, exspire, perspire, respire.) The etymological meaning of that is *to breathe together*. I would just like to close by saying, let us continue to conspire to protest.

CT: Thank you, Joe.

A reverence for life

An interview with Vimala Thakar
San Francisco, U.S.A.

We are the weavers of the fabric of modern society.
We can weave love, truthfulness and peace
or we can weave hatred, mistrust and war.
We will have to wear whatever fabric we weave

In some of the traditions of the East, the spiritual teacher may rarely refer to her or his personal history. It is as if the particular events and experiences shaping and weaving that person's life do not matter and could even be harmful to the listener who might live in awe and wonder of the teacher's life.

I was reminded of this when attempting to glean information about Vimala Thakar, an international speaker on spiritual, social and global values. Despite the numerous books which she has had published, including *The Eloquence of Living, Spirituality and Social Action, Meditation – A Way of Life* and *The Mystery of Silence*, there is barely a sentence in them of information about herself. Similarly, in her public talks, unusually free of a religious ideology and language, she does not touch upon her past, no doubt because she recognises that the totality of the present is what matters.

I even wrote to one of her groups of friends and supporters around the world and they regretfully replied that they did not possess any biographical information.

In the winter of 1956, Vimala Thakar from Maharashtra in India, went to visit Krishnamurti in Varanasi. She had studied philosophy, understood Sanskirt and had a wide variety of religious experiences. Prior to meeting Krishnamurti, she had walked through the villages of India to reclaim land for the landless under Vinoba Bhave. Vimala became friends with Krishnamurti and listened to his teachings, not only in India but also in London and Saanen, Switzerland. When Vimala became deaf in one ear in 1960 she was said to have been healed through Krishnamurti placing his hands on her head, an uncharacteristic expression by the man.

People at some of Krishnamurti's gatherings that Vimala attended appreciated her insights and wisdom whenever she got into informal conversations with other participants. Out of these small meetings came invitations for her to speak in Holland and other parts of the world. In India she actively promoted the Vinoba Bhave Land Gift Movement and currently, the Jeevan Yoga Foundation for village self-sufficiency.

One of the characteristic features of Vimala is that she has refused to follow any of the traditional paths of spirituality. She says that human beings need to be 'vitally committed' to the discovery of truth and delving to the roots of social injustice.

In her book *Spirituality and Social Action*, she writes:

> *Living is something which is done in totality.*
> *A flower which is blossoming unfolds every petal.*
> *The beauty and the scent which were hidden in the bud*
> *come out completely.*
> *A fruit when it ripens grows ripe in totality.*
> *But we human beings grow partially in fragments.*
> *If we have the urge to live fully, totally,*
> *as marvelous, complete, mature expressions of humanity,*
> *we must meet life sensitively, alertly*
> *with each day that dawns.*

I met with Vimala in a small house in San Francisco. She was facilitating camps in the United States, where people would spend several days with her, listening to talks, inquiring into the nature of things and spending periods in meditative reflection. She has held such camps at her home in Mount Abu, India, and in Europe, Australia and South America.

She gives the appearance of smallness and frailty but this belies her presence. She is an eloquent speaker, both privately and publicly, both of the words she speaks and that which is beyond words.

> *When we explore life's wholeness, untouched by words,*
> *when we live in its freshness, its limitlessness,*
> *we see for ourselves the sacred, the holy,*
> *without which life has no meaning.*

CT: What is the importance of observation and what does this mean in daily life?

VT: We need to observe what is happening to our minds while we move through relationships. It is only through observation that you understand what is happening inside. Understanding requires encounter with facts and observation leads you to the perception of facts.

CT: If in my observation I see the fact, I might say, 'Well, I observe the fact of my anxiety, my fear, my possessiveness, but it doesn't seem to make a great deal of difference to the fact. Why isn't it changing or fading away?'

VT: Most probably you aren't allowing it to fade away. We justify the existence of our weaknesses in the name of psychology. We justify and defend it and thereby we prevent it from dropping away.

CT: So one must be willing to let go.

VT: Yes. Then one would become a religious inquirer. A religious inquirer is one who is willing to discover the truth and not allow anything to come between the truth and oneself. That is being religious.

CT: We can be willing to let go and yet it can still remain extraordinarily difficult.

VT: What kind of difficulty?

CT: Psychological pain, emotional pain, confusion, fear. So I wonder if there are any other factors which essentially contribute to this letting go upon seeing the fact.

VT: I think if there is purification on the physical level through proper diet, simple living, austerity in speech and so on, there will be sensitivity. Without this preparation, the event of dropping away of age-old weaknesses and distortions doesn't take place. It can't happen. That's why self-education is necessary. When there is an urge for personal discovery of truth I think the quality of religiousness gets activated. Religion is a personal discovery.

CT: You are saying one has to see for oneself, not get it secondhand. How can one safeguard oneself against not becoming dependent on you or on others who are speaking about the realities of life? That always seems to happen in religious life.

VT: It happens in religious life if one wants the easy way of accepting authority and escaping from the responsibility of personal observation and discovery. If you want the easy way then you go and follow someone and fall in the trap. What is more important is the love of freedom, the desire to exercise one's own initiative and not to bargain and give away your freedom for anything.

CT: So your function is to put the focus back on the person.

VT: That's right. Lead a person toward his or her inner life; not make them dependent upon me.

CT: Would you say there are far too few teachers who do that? The tendency seems to be towards dependency, authority, religious leaders, gurus, and so on.

VT: This commercialization of religion and spirituality is the curse of the day. We are living in a commercialized civilization. So religion and spirituality are also misused, abused. A new relationship between the inquirer and the person who understands is necessary.

CT: What are the dynamics of a balanced relationship?

VT: I have used the term 'the non-authoritarian way', which I use to refer to a way of communication. I communicate with you and you communicate with me in a non-authoritarian way. A simple person who has arrived at enlightenment can be misused by those who are craving to find an authority. They become dependent and relegate the responsibility to that person. That is our pattern of life.

We have to stimulate the urge for freedom, an urge for learning. If we can stimulate these two things among the people we come across then they will know that freedom is something which cannot be bargained for. You know, freedom is not something you sell and then get something in return for, not even liberation and enlightenment. The transpsychological value of freedom should be emphasized as well as respect and a reverence for life. These are the essential things.

CT: I would like to go back to observation and meditation. In observation, the heart and mind come to quietness rather naturally or effortlessly. And there comes within that movement a meditative state of being.

VT: I would say silence rather than meditation. Between meditation and a state of observation comes the dimension of silence, a total emptiness. So observation leads to that total emptiness. Silence is the dimension of innumerable energies. Modern man is so fatigued and exhausted, even for a man with a cultivated mind. Before he can act in the so-called outer or social field he has to discover in his being a new energy. The dimension of silence provides one with the release of such energies.

CT: Taking the example of a monk's life, the monk leads a rather simple life with a certain purity of speech and an awareness of diet.

The monk observes and is aware of his relationship to the world and there is a quietness in his life. Monks come to a certain silence and emptiness, perhaps, either through the absence of method and technique or not. Energies may get released yet they may not be visibly manifesting in the world.

VT: What do the monks do, then?

CT: Live very quietly and simply. Some monks live in total isolation and some are in a monastic setting.

VT: That's not living. Once you remove yourself from the mainstream of relationships and withdraw into isolation, physical or psychological, you have stopped living.

CT: Are you saying that the monastic system in which monks and nuns live is inadequate?

VT: They create an artificial world. They create a world for themselves and live there. If you withdraw for the sake of study, investigation and exploration one can understand that. But if you create a pattern of isolation, whether it is monastic life or any other life, you cut yourself away from the challenges of life and relationships. Western or Eastern, in every setting, the desire for security keeps people isolated mentally.

CT: So what will contribute to our being less isolated?

VT: It is the willingness to be vulnerable to life, whatever it brings; to meet life. Living is to move with the challenges of life. Meditation can give us a greater capacity to meet these challenges. So it is vitally necessary to go into retreat. We need to wash out all the toxins that get into our psyche when we are exposed to the inhumane stress and strain of modern life. Usually people go out for vacations. If instead they go out for retreats they will come back revitalized and re-energized, provided they do not fall into the trap of any sect or dogma.

CT: In a way this is a new and refreshing approach – to step out of the 'world' for short periods. It's not like the life-long monastic system but it is short-term. One is nourished so that one can live clearly in the world.

VT: Yes. It's like inhalation and exhalation. You inhale vital breath when you go into retreat or occasional silence. You are inhaling the energies. Then when you go back to your relationships and your so-called 'world', you are exhaling. So it's a cycle of inhaling and exhaling.

CT: In giving consideration to the total sphere of life, you include political action.

VT: Not power politics but people politics.

CT: Would a person need to include this dimension if one's life is to be total?

VT: Not artificially. Everything gets included according to one's inclination. Somebody may be an artist and they will function through their art. Somebody may be a musician and they will utilize their capacities. And the same with literature, dance, economics and political work.

Through silence and meditation the centre of the 'me' disappears completely. You are nothing but emptiness covered by flesh and bones. Then it is life universal which uses such a person according to its capacities, strengths, talents, etc. It is not for the person to decide what course of action he or she will take. Life brings to the doorstep the field of action.

CT: So, out of the emptiness, there comes such a degree of receptivity that one doesn't actually have to look.

VT: That's right. One doesn't have to choose. It comes.

CT: For people involved in peace work, one of the difficulties is the degree of aggression and negativity of some of the people involved.

VT: Then it's not peace work. If the minds of the workers are not peaceful then they don't know that peace is a total way of living. If the peace has not altered the quality of their motivations and the texture of their behaviour, then they are not peace workers. The existing peace movements may not have a spiritual foundation. Every action should have a spiritual foundation, or ego-less consciousness, or the dimension of awareness. They will have to find out ways and means of working for peace. Then they will be working out of compassion and not out of any ambition.

CT: Would you say that, in a total sense, work on oneself is a prerequisite to outer work?

VT: Absolutely so.

CT: Some may say that it is a prerequisite to be a totally prepared human being. But the world is in such a crisis and in such danger, should I keep preparing myself or should I bring the inner and outer work together?

VT: I think the person is under some illusion. While I am preparing myself for mutation, or transformation, I am contributing to the world of peace. The very act of self-education is an act of tremendous service to humanity. When one human being transcends the bondage of the ego, or 'I' consciousness, they become a living cell of something new which is going to spread from their centre. So it is not that while you are preparing yourself your are not contributing. There is no dichotomy between the two.

CT: I agree. But the structure of society says that unless you are seen to be visibly doing something then you are not contributing. This is a Western idea.

VT: That's the problem of society; that's not our problem.

CT: Vimalaji, what would you say are the factors in daily life which contribute to transformation? For example, how important do you consider contact with like-minded people?

VT: If the religious inquiry becomes the common point which brings people together then I think it will be very wholesome. How do you create that contact with like-minded people in daily living? How do they come together? What will be the basis? Is there a person or an ideology around which they will rally? Or will the like-minded persons or inquirers come together only because they are inquirers?

There is the necessity for such people coming together and we have to function in this man-made world. So if we get one another's support, moral and psychological, it becomes easier for us. But how do the people come together?

Up to now they have been coming together around a person. They are more with one person than with one another. So individuals are rallying around a person, around an ideology in the framework of an organization or sect. But free individuals as inquirers or religious persons coming together in freedom, on the basis of friendship and common inquiry, is something which is not seen in the world.

CT: To some degree people rally to you, not necessarily as an authority figure, or as a cult or sect, but they still rally to you. Without someone who has deeper understanding, can people really rally with each other?

VT: That's my hope. For tomorrow.

CT: Would you say that meditation is an absolute essential for clear action even though fears arise when we see the tendencies of mind and when we go into the unknown?

VT: Meditation is a way of living.

CT: Therefore, it is neither inner or outer.

VT: That's right. It's total. It's a totality that moves within, in relationship to a totality that is outside of you.

CT: Often the mind creates the idea of seeing the totality in a passive way and not an appreciation of the active quality of being in the totality. How do we come to an understanding that it is not just seeing totality as a meditation state?

VT: Totality is often regarded as a rigid destination. But it's a beginning of new life where there is no division of the 'me' and the 'not-me'. There is a quality of a new perception and quite a different quality of responses. So the movement of totality means the movement of egolessness.

People have created an entity out of totality, out of God, out of liberation. As if there is something out there to reach. But it is not a fixed point, not at all.

CT: Beautiful. Thank you, Vimalaji.

A postscript from the author

There is a wide body of contemporary and traditional spiritual teachings which serve the genuine interests of all forms of life. We might explore some of the following themes in our daily life. The relationship to each of these themes have widespread consequences. Let us wake up to the challenge.

1. To reject any livelihood or investment which is threatening or destructive to people, animals or the environment and to create useful activities whether one is employed or not.

2. To apply genuine moderation in lifestyle and to make possessions last.

3. To give up eating animals, including birds and fish.

4. To regard all events and experiences, no matter how painful, as a learning experience.

5. To abide in mindfulness and awareness through the cycle of our daily activities.

6. To explore contact with like-minded people through friends, meetings, conferences, travel, workshops and retreats.

7. To value being over having, sharing over taking, letting go over grabbing hold of; openness over withdrawal; non-violent struggle over apathy.

8. To give regularly in cash or kind or both to some of the wide range of individuals, groups, organizations and charities who are expressing wisdom and compassion.

9. In political matters to be free from clinging to the narrow ideology of the left, right and centre; to instead question, 'Where is the compassion? Where are the peace-making activities? Where is the genuine concern for people, animals and environment?' – and actively support such an emphasis.

10. To be receptive to the joys of life – in oneself, in others, in nature, in being creative, in the arts, in awareness, insight and freedom – and to celebrate the wonders and mysteries of life.

Christopher Titmuss is a member of:

Action on Smoking and Health, 5–11 Mortimer Street, London W1N 7RH.

Amnesty International, 5 Roberts Place, off Bowling Green Lane, London EC1 DEJ.

Animal Aid, 7 Castle Street, Tonbridge, Kent.

Buddhist Peace Fellowship, 8 West Allington, Bridport, Dorset DT6 5BG.

Campaign for Nuclear Disarmament, 22 Underwood Street, London N1 7JG.

Friends of the Earth, 26 Underwood Street, London N1 7JQ.

Green Party, 10 Station Parade, Balham High Road, London SW12 9AZ.

Greenpeace, 30–31 Islington Green, London N1 8XE.

Insight Meditation Society, Barre, Mass. 01005, USA.

International Network of Engaged Buddhists, 303/7 Santipop Nares Road, Bankok, 10500, Thailand.

OXFAM, (Oxford Committee for Famine Relief), 274 Banbury Road, Oxford OX2 7DZ.

Schumacher Society, Ford House, Hartland, Bideford, Devon EX39 6EE.

Survival International, 310 Edgware Road, London W2 1DY.

Vegetarian Society, Parkdale, Altrincham, Cheshire WA14 4QG.

War on Want, 37 Great Guildford Street, London SE1.